SEEN ON THE PACKHORSE TRACKS

SEEN ON THE PACKHORSE TRACKS

TITUS THORNBER

SOUTH PENNINE PACKHORSE TRAILS TRUST

Published by the South Pennine Packhorse Trails Trust
The Barn, Mankinholes, Todmorden OL14 6HR
A registered charity no. 1001929

Printed in Great Britain by Pennine Printing Services Ltd
Unit 6, Commercial Mills, Oldham Road, Ripponden,
West Yorkshire HX6 4EH

ISBN 0 95 30573 2 1 hardback
ISBN 0 95 30573 3 X paperback

Contents

Subscribers   vii

Acknowledgements   ix

Foreword by Lady Towneley   xi

Introduction by Sue Hogg   xiii

Chapter 1   The Terrain   1

Chapter 2   Packhorse Bridges   9

Chapter 3   Culverts and Fords   22

Chapter 4   Causeways   26

Chapter 5   Holloways and Ridgeways   33

Chapter 6   Peatlands   39

Chapter 7   Waymarks, Signposts and Cairns   46

Chapter 8   Gateposts, Ginnels and Turnbyes   54

Chapter 9   Overnight Stopping Places   62

Chapter 10   The Inclosure of the Commons   67

Chapter 11   Packhorse Vocabulary   73

Chapter 12   The South Pennine Packhorse Trails Trust   80

Glossary   89

Further Reading   93

Gazetteer   94

Index   97

Subscribers

Mrs Josie Angelo-Sparling
Lord & Lady Ashbrook, Arley Charitable Trust
Bill & Elizabeth Barrett
Mr & Mrs Lawrence W. Burton
Betty Byrne
Susan Carter
Elizabeth L. Colquhoun
Bev Corrigan
Christine Delves
George Dickinson MH, MFH
Carole England
Sebastian di Ferranti Trust
Miss Theresa Fitzherbert
Mrs M. Fletcher
Roger Barstow Frost MBE, MA
John P. B. Golding, Morep Food Processing Systems
Mr R. A. Greenaway
Eric Greenwood
Tony Greenwood
Mr & Mrs T. L. Halstead
Kit Hardwick
Mrs J. R. S. Heaton
Hebden Bridge Literary and Scientific Society,
  Local History Section
Dr M. C. Higham
Miss C. M. Hill
Reg Hindley

Professor James Hogg
Howarth & Oxenhope District Bridleways Group
Stephen & Gaynor Irvine
Maggie Jones
Mr J. D. Kay
Alan Kind, Hodology Ltd
Lady Kirk
Michael F. Leonard
Nicholas Oliver Livsey
Pat McCloskey, United Utilities
Dr W. R. Mitchell MBE
D. Michael Morgan, Adam F. Greenhalgh & Co.
John R. Murray Esq
Terry Norris
John Oldham
Mrs Vicky Ord
Christine Peat
James Pickering
Mary-Jo Pinder
Ramblers' Association, North East Lancashire Area
Ramblers' Association, Burnley & Pendle Group
George Ramsden, Stone Trough Books
Brain Rich
Rochdale, Bury Bridleways Association
Sue Rogers
Miss Margaret Rooker
David & Ella Rowe

Subscribers

Miss J. R. Rowell
Sue Rumfitt Associates
David Shore
Richard Smith
Mr F. Tattersall
Mr & Mrs David M. Tattersall
Jean Tennant

Colonel John Bradford Timmins OBE, TD, JP
Sir Simon Towneley KCVO
Miss Cosima Towneley
Miss Sandra Twigg
Whitworth Historical Society Museum
Iain A. Williamson

Acknowledgements

Many people have contributed towards the production of this book. For their generous financial support the South Pennine Packhorse Trails Trust would like to thank the Fort Foundation, the Foundation for Sport and the Arts, the J. Paul Getty Charitable Trust, the Idlewild Trust, Lord Leverhulme's Charitable Trust, David and Ella Rowe, and the Scouloudi Foundation. Thanks also to the extremely patient subscribers listed on pp. vii-viii. The Trust is also grateful to the Mrs Elise Pilkington Charitable Trust for its continuing support.

To those who have provided information and/or pictures, who have commented on the text and helped with proof-reading, and who have kindly given us permission to reproduce illustrations, our thanks. They are Roger Birch, Sue Carter, Roy Deane, Christine Delves, Anne Foster, John Golding, Tony Greenwood, John Hodgson, Abigail Hogg, Dr W. R. Mitchell MBE, Diana Monahan, Brian Perkins, Mike Russell, John Sharples, Ken Spencer, Tim Stevens and Simon Warner. And special thanks are due to Frank Woolrych, who kindly spent so much time scanning the illustrations.

And finally, we owe a great debt of gratitude to the late Mary Towneley, who, although very ill, shortly before her death wrote to the subscribers.

Illustration credits

Every effort has been made to trace copyright holders. The publishers apologize if any have inadvertently been overlooked and ask them to contact us.

Alice Longstaff Gallery Collection: 77
Roger Birch: xxii
Allen Butterfield: xxi (left)
Roy Deane: 63
Christine Delves: 26
Carole England: 86 (bottom)
W. Gilbert Foster: 76
Sam Gibson: 48
S. Greenwood: 15
Hebden Bridge Literary & Scientific Society, Local History Collection: 15, 48 (right), 56 (bottom), 65, 76
Canon Harry W. Hodgson: 37 (top & bottom), 50 (left & centre)
Sue Hogg: front cover, inside front cover, xv, xxi (right), 1, 2, 3 (left), 4, 5, 10, 11, 13, 14, 16, 18, 19, 23, 27, 29 (bottom), 30, 35 (left), 36, 38, 41 (top & bottom), 42, 47, 49, 50 (right), 51, 52, 55 (left & top right), 56 (top), 59, 61 (left & right), 69, 71 (left & right), 74, 78, 85 (left & bottom right), 86 (top)

Acknowledgements

David Mansell: 85 (top right)
James Maxim: 44, 79
Thomas Morgan: 65
Jonathan Ogilvie: 12, 21 (top), 22, 24, 29 (top), 54, 57
Pendle Archaeology Group: 32, 40
Brian Perkins: 21 (bottom)
Mike Russell: 39
Titus Thornber: back cover, xiii, xiv, 20, 25, 33, 34, 46, 48 (left), 58, 62 (left & right), 70, 73
Simon Warner: 28
Robert Watson: 3 (right)
Mike Williams: 55 (bottom)
Frank Woolrych: xx

Production credits
Designer: Jonathan Ogilvie
Editor: Sue Hogg

Foreword

For hundreds of years packhorses were an integral part of everyday life, as familiar to the cottager as to the castle-dweller, and the trails they used were vital to tradesman and traveller alike. The early industrial development of this country was nurtured by the transport of goods carried on the sturdy backs of the teams steadily winding their way over the inhospitable and remote uplands between the growing cities along miry roads unfit for wheeled traffic.

Today the needs they serviced are covered by the travelling salesman and fleets of articulated lorries thundering across the country on an ever expanding web of tarmac. The welcome jingle of bells announcing the approach of the packman and his team has been replaced by the constant roar of the internal combustion engine, and the well-established pattern of green tracks now lies fragmented and forgotten, often buried under the spreading industrial developments that they once fed.

Titus Thornber has dedicated many years to rediscovering these hidden highways and researching their use. In doing so he has made a remarkable contribution to our knowledge of the packhorse routes, the features seen upon them and the countryside through which they run. Readers of this book will not only be fascinated by the wealth of information it contains but will, I feel sure, be inspired to explore for themselves the hidden world which it discovers. They will want to ride or walk in the footsteps of Ailse O'Fussers and her team of 'lime gals', mindful of the inscription on the tomb of packman Christopher Duckworth above Haslingden, 'loving his horses, by his horses loved'.

I hope that it will also encourage all who read it to support the work of the South Pennine Packhorse Trails Trust which is helping to save what is left of these historic bridleroads for future generations, as a continuing thread of gold in the living tapestry of the Pennines.

Mary Towneley
Dyneley
Cliviger

Introduction

When Titus Thornber asked me to write the introduction to this book, which he has written as a gift to the Packhorse Trails Trust, I felt it was a considerable honour. There are two reasons for this: first, the fact that Titus considered the Trust worthy of a present such as this, and second, compared to him I am an absolute beginner as a collector of packhorse tracks.

However, the book has grown into something of a collaboration, for over the years the Trust has accumulated a collection of pictures, many of which illustrate exactly the points that Titus is making. It has been a matter of fitting words and images together.

In the process, this venture has turned out to be a voyage of discovery. I have always preferred to explore the countryside on horseback, and am convinced – rightly or wrongly – that it is the only way to appreciate fully the logic of the packhorse roads. They went the way they went for good reason, and it is only on horseback that that becomes apparent.

Also, it is a much less strenuous way to travel. One doesn't have to spend the whole time looking where one is putting one's feet – the pony does the work, the rider can sit back and study the landscape as it unfolds. When walking, it is necessary to stop to admire the view. Cycling suffers the same disadvantage, and looks to be such hard work besides.

In the course of working on the book, Titus and I

TITUS AND FAMILY AT LUMB FALLS, CRIMSWORTH DEAN

STOPPING TO ADMIRE THE VIEW ON LONG CAUSEWAY, LANGFIELD COMMON

made several joint expeditions, and in the quest for specific features I have had to explore on foot those trails that are no longer accessible on horseback. It has been a most enjoyable voyage of discovery, and that is in part the book's underlying purpose: to help people find for themselves what is there on the ground. The fascination lies as much in the search as the goal.

As an engineer, Titus has concentrated on the shape and form of the packhorse tracks in the landscape, and explains how they were built and why they are like they are. But, behind what is visible now, there lies a past thronged with the shades of travellers who, down the centuries, used these ways to go about their everyday business in much the same way that we do today, although now we travel by motorised vehicle – whether car, lorry, bus or train. For the commuters and long-distance drivers of the past, the engine that moved them was the horse, and particularly the packhorse, who for centuries was the main means of carrying goods around the country. And trade was considerable. In the 1720s Daniel Defore reported that such great quantities of cloth were sent from

Yorkshire and Lancashire to Stourbridge Fair in Cambridgeshire that nearly a thousand horses were needed to convey it, and to bring back vast quantities of hops. So great was the woollen industry in Yorkshire that raw wool was imported from East Anglia on horseback.

It was not only packhorse teams that thronged the highways. Herds of cattle, sheep and pigs were driven from all over the country to the London markets – 40,000 Highland cattle travelled south each year to be fattened in Norfolk. In the autumn, after the harvest, droves of geese, up to two thousand at a time, would journey from Suffolk, grazing on the stubble as they went. In 1750 some 150,000 turkeys crossed the Stour at Stratford Bridge on the long march to London.

But packhorse transport is much older than the eighteenth century, and encompassed the whole country. Along the line of packhorse routes it is possible to find remnants of Bronze Age walling, with megaliths or boulders that mark the boundaries of settlements some three thousand years old. And orthostatic walls, with their elongated stones, range in age from three hundred to three thousand years.

The earliest written record of a causeway – the characteristic style of construction for packhorse trails in the Pennines – that I have come across relates to the road over Blackstone Edge between Rochdale and Elland. In 1291 Hugh of Elland was granted the right to levy tolls on goods carried over the Edge, the money to be spent on repairing the causeway. This would have been highly lucrative monopoly, for the causeway was part of the main road between York and Chester in medieval times. In the seventeenth century the Sowerby Constables' records reveal a picture of travel along this great highway unequalled in all

ORTHOSTATIC WALL, WITH ELONGATED STONES, BUILT ON AN EMBANKMENT ALONGSIDE AN ANCIENT WAY LEADING TO THE MEDIEVAL SETTLEMENT OF LOWER RAWTONSTALL, ABOVE CHARLESTOWN, HEBDEN BRIDGE

England, with links from Chester to Ireland, according to the Halifax historian, W. B. Crump. In 1675 it was mapped as a principal cross road by the King's Cosmographer John Ogilby, and in the following century Daniel Defoe tells us that its ultimate destinations were Hull and Plymouth.

The causeway repaired by Hugh of Elland in the 1290s could be the great stone track that crosses from Lancashire into Yorkshire just east of Littleborough. This stretch is claimed to be a Roman road, but so are many old roads that never saw a Roman. If it is Hugh's road, it is much more interesting to a packhorse trail collector, for whom Roman roads do not have the same appeal. The Normans were skilled in building in stone and would have been more than capable of constructing such a road. Indeed, there are many features in common between the early gritstone tracks of the mid-Pennines and the granite tracks of Normandy. The other explanation for the great causeway – put forward by the Rochdale historian James Maxim – is that it is the first turnpike road across Blackstone Edge, built in the 1730s.

So many of these routes are very ancient, and have seen a great deal of traffic, which increased over the centuries.

In the Northern and Midland counties, the single pony which had borne, to the Leeds cloth-market, the weekly produce of the little farmer-clothier, gradually developed into long strings of pack-horses to and from every industrial centre, passing, in some frequented thoroughfares, in an almost continuous stream [Sidney and Beatrice Webb, *The Story of the King's Highway*, p. 64].

By the seventeenth and eighteenth centuries strings of packhorses carrying bursting packs of merchandise plied the Great North Road on their way to London. In Staffordshire 'pack-horses and asses, heavily laden with coal, . . . tubs full of ground flint from the mills, crates of ware or panniers of clay, [floundered] knee-deep through muddy holes and ruts that was all but impassable' (*Life of Josiah Wedgwood*, quoted by the Webbs, op. cit., p. 64).

Even during the Civil War clothier Thomas Priestley made regular journeys from Goodgreave in Soyland to Blackwell Hall, the cloth exchange in London, with a small team of Galloway ponies carrying home-

MEDIEVAL PACKHORSES BEING USED FOR CARRYING WATER *(top left)* AND CORN *(above)* (*The Luttrell Psalter*, 1320-40)

produced cloth, although at times he hired a guard for protection.

It was not only packhorses that thronged the highways but heavy wagons and carts, churning up soft soils into a boggy mass of ruts. In 1675 Thomas Mace published a pamphlet, which he sent to Charles II, with suggestions for improving the roads in the kingdom, and for reducing the stress engendered in the poor traveller having to negotiate bad roads and cope with bad behaviour. He suggested a 'smart Law' should be passed 'to keep all irregular and troublesome persons in an orderly way of Civility in their Travel':

That no man should be pestered by giving the way (sometimes) to hundreds of Pack-horses, Panniers, Whifflers, Coaches, Waggons, Wains, Carts, or whatsoever others, which continually are very grievous to weary and loaden Travellers; but more especially near the City and upon a Market-day, a man having travelld a long and tedious Journey, his Horse well nigh spent, shall sometimes be compelld to cross out of his way twenty times in one mile's Riding . . . [Thomas Mace, . . . *A short Rational Discourse, . . . Concerning the High-ways of ENGLAND: Their Badness, the Causes thereof, the Reasons of those Causes, the impossibility of ever having them Well-mended according the Old Way of mending.* Printed for the Public good in the Year 1675].

It was in the same year that John Ogilby published *Britannia*, the first set of road maps showing, in strip form, the principal highways of the country.

In the Pennines the roads were possibly better made than in other parts of the country, because stone was always plentifully available for road building. The advent of the turnpike trusts brought great improvements, making the roads more suitable for wheeled vehicles, by widening them and by reducing the gradients. The first turnpike Act for Blackstone Edge was passed 1734, and other roads were turnpiked over the next few decades. The earliest turnpikes were mainly improved packhorse tracks, and bore little resemblance to what we now think of as roads. Even so, by 1775 the Reverend John Watson could write:

it is amazing to think under what disadvantages the trade of the country must formerly have been carried on, before the roads were repaired, and widened, by

A VICTORIAN REPRESENTATION OF A SIXTEENTH-CENTURY PACKHORSE TRAIN TRAVELLING THROUGH THE PENNINES. UNUSUALLY, EACH PONY HAS A SET OF BELLS, APART FROM THE LEADER (engraving by Louis Huard, from Samuel Smiles, *Lives of the Engineers*, 1860-61)

different Acts of Parliament which have lately been obtained; for they not only were narrow and rugged, but laid out seemingly without any regard to the ease of cattle, or the expedition of transacting business, for they sometimes went by the very steepest part of hills, when the road would have been shorter, if it had missed them. . . . Since trade has increased so prodigiously, and so great a number of carriages are used, . . . as great improvements are now making in different parts of this parish, as almost any other country can shew [*History and Antiquities of the Parish of Halifax*, pp. 7-8].

It is difficult now to appreciate the speed of the packhorse trains and the distances they covered. In the early seventeeth century fish was transported from Lyme Regis to London by what can only be described as packhorse express.

Horses with panniers called dorsers were taken onto the beach tied one to the other ready to receive the fish. When the dorsers were filled, the driver mounted the foremost horse of the train, and galloped off to London [Webbs, op. cit., p. 66].

And, so the Webbs record, in 1710 'no fewer than 320 fish-laden horses' galloped through Tunbridge every day on their way to London.

Flying teams of packhorses presented something of a hazard to other travellers. The following account by agriculturalist Charles Vancouver, published in 1813, describes packhorses in Devon:

It is truly suprising to see with what speed and security the native horses of the county will pass over . . . rough and broken places, whether burthened or otherwise . . . The rapidity with which a gang of packhorses descend the hills, when not loaded, and the utter impossibility of passing loaded ones, require that the utmost caution should be used in keeping out of the way of the one and

exertion in keeping ahead of the other. A crossway fork in the road or gateway is eagerly looked for as a retiring spot for the traveller, until the passing squadron or heavily loaded brigade, may have passed by [quoted in David Hey, *Packmen, Carriers and Packhorse Roads*, pp. 87-8].

In upland areas packhorses could cover at least 30 miles a day fully laden. Ruth Ryder, a descendant of a family of carriers who lived in Briercliffe in east Lancashire in the early nineteenth century, gives the following account of a typical journey:

Some of the family lived at Flout [Float] Bridge [in Trawden] and kept three gangs of horses. One of the family . . . told me once that they used to start at Flout Bridge and go down to Marsden [near Colne] and load coal on the horses' backs and take it to Lothersdale lime kilns, load lime there and come home, unload there and start again the morning after and come over Widdop Head down to Hebble End [at Hebden Bridge], and then up that road under the arch above Weasel Hall, across Bell House Moor, and so forward to Saddleworth, leave the lime there and then to Huddersfield to load wheat for the Burnley corn mills, a three-day journey [information kindly supplied by Ken Spencer].

As the crow flies, this three-day journey works out at 83 miles.

Carriers operated over long distances. According to Janet Withersby, twelve Kendalmen were recorded in the Stratford on Avon guild registers between 1406 and 1535, and of these five were also trading in Southampton. And John Hanworth of Bury, a clothier who died in 1570, directed in his will that 20 shillings should be left to the curates or clergy of every village on the way to London, the money to be used for relief

WEAVERS TAKING THEIR PIECES TO MARKET (George Walker, *Costume of Yorkshire*, 1814). HEPTONSTALL, COLNE, HUDDERSFIELD AND HALIFAX EACH HAD A CLOTH OR PIECE HALL

of the poor. He was also one of several packhorse men to leave money for road repair or improvement, including '£10 to gain interest for 1 year then to maintain roads in Bury and Bolton'.

The standard weight for a packload can be worked out from the old saying 'A penny a pound, a pound a pack.' This needs explanation in these times of decimalization. A penny (1d) is the old penny in pounds, shillings and pence, with 240d (pence) to the pound (£1). Thus, if a pound in weight (1 lb) cost 1d, and a packhorse load cost £1, it must have weighed 240 lb or 17 stone, nearly 109 kilos. This is equivalent to carrying a fairly hefty man, no mean feat in terrain with gradients of 1 in 3.

According to Anthony Dent and Daphne Machin

Goodall, the favoured breed for packhorses was the Galloway, from southwest Scotland, 'a breed of small, elegant horses . . . similar to those of Iceland and Sweden, . . . the best of which sometimes reached the height of fourteen hands and a half,' according to a Dr Anderson, writing in the eighteenth century. 'In point of elegance of shape it was a perfect picture; and in disposition was gentle and compliant.'

Galloways were famed for their stamina. They were described as 'right hardy workers who could take their place among the heaviest breeds in almost any work on the farm. . . . There was nothing striking about them except their movement which was easy and rapid with great staying power, [they] could run twelve to fifteen miles or more without breaking trot.'

The breed was particularly suited to hill country: 'Its qualities were speed, stoutness, and surefootedness over a very rugged and mountainous country.' Galloways were the basic racing stock in earliest times and throughout the Middle Ages.

Sadly the breed is now extinct in Britain; in Scotland it was crossed with Clydesdales to produce a larger horse. However, it continues to make its contribution to equine bloodlines, for Galloway mares were used as the foundation stock of the English Thoroughbred. The breed may still survive in South America, for Galloway ponies were exported there in the eighteenth century (Anthony Dent and Daphne Machin

Goodall, *The Foals of Epona*, 1962, pp. 218-19).

An intriguing find in the course of working on this book is a photograph of possibly the last Galloway in the country. It comes from a 3-volume book entitled *The Horse*, edited by Professor J. Wortley Axe and published in 1908. The entry on 'The Packhorse' records that a pair of Galloways from Devon were displayed at the Crystal Palace Horse Show in 1897. The accompanying photograph shows 'Packhorse Triumph II'. Whether a true Galloway or a Devonshire packhorse, a strain which possibly derived from the Galloway, Triumph II fits the descriptions of Galloways quoted above. For example, he is clean-legged, unlike the Dales or Fell.

'Galloway' became a generic term for a packhorse. Frequently it was shortened to 'gal'. Hence 'lime gals' were not young women, but packhorses carrying lime.

The skill of driving teams of packhorses, as many as 30 or 40 animals at a time, has been lost, but in his *General History of Quadrupeds* (1790) Thomas Bewick gives some insights into what packhorsing entailed:

In their journeys over the trackless moors, they strictly adhere to the line of order and regularity custom has taught them to observe: the leading Horse, which is always chosen for his sagacity and steadiness, being furnished with bells, gives notice to the rest, which follow the sound, and generally without much deviation, though sometimes at a considerable distance. The following anecdote will shew with what obstinate perseverance they have been known to observe their line of order: – Some years ago, one of these Horses, which had been long accustomed to follow his leader, by accident or fatigue was thrown into an inferior rank: the poor animal, as if sensible of his disgrace, by the most strenuous exertions, at length recovered his usual station, which he maintained during the remainder of the journey; but on his arrival in the inn-yard, he dropped down dead upon the spot, his life falling a sacrifice to his ambition.

It is the bidability and willingness of the horse to work as part of a team, whether with humans or other horses, that made it so ideal for carrying goods over long distances. This is evident in an account of packhorsing in the Pennines in the nineteenth century:

PACKHORSE TRIUMPH II – THE LAST OF THE GALLOWAYS?

A gang of galloways consisted of 12-14 horses. They always walked in single file, the first horse wearing a collar of bells and known as the bell-horse. They set off at 4 a. m., each horse with a pack on its back, secured there by a wanta – a broad webbing belt, with ropes and hooks at both ends. First the webbing went round the horse for ease, then the ropes went over the pack, under the horse and fastened to the hooks. When light flagstones or slates were required to be carried, a hook-seam was attached to the pack-saddle by means of a staple.

After starting the horses would generally be allowed to eat grass by the roadside or open spaces, as they went along; but the drivers when they considered they had had sufficient, would put on muzzles, which were like those of dogs, only a little more square. If the bell-horse, while grazing, happened to get behind the others, as soon as it was muzzled it knew the real travelling for the day had commenced, and would bore and push until its own honoured place as leader was gained.

The bells it wore were seven, one ordinary shaped bell in the middle and three round ones on each side. These had a small slit in the bottom, through which a little

WOODEN PACKSADDLE, BROAD BOTTOM FARM, MYTHOLMROYD. THIS ONE STILL HAS ITS PADDING AND PART OF THE BREECHING WHICH PREVENTS THE LOAD FROM SLIPPING FORWARD WHEN GOING DOWNHILL

molten metal had been passed to form a tongue. The bells were fixed to a leather collar, which was fastened to the top of the pack-saddle and hung loosely across the shoulders, so that they rang with every movement of the horse. Occasionally the men would walk ahead a mile or so, in order to have a pint or a pipe at some well-known pub. The gals understood this proceeding, and (if they were muzzled) would jog along as if their drivers were by their sides.

If the drivers were going on more than one day's journey, they would put up for the night at some wayside inn. First they would unfasten the wantas, throw down the packs in a sheltered yard, take off the muzzles and turn the horses into the croft or paddock. Next day they would be away again very early [S. Emily Lumb, *North Country Lore and Legend,* September 1890, p. 397].

EIGHTEENTH CENTURY PACKHORSE BELLS

IN THE MID-PENNINES FARM COBS CONTINUED TO BE USED INTO THE TWENTIETH CENTURY FOR LOCAL DELIVERIES. THIS PICTURE WAS TAKEN *circa* 1905-10

The large teams of packhorses ceased to operate as long-distance carriers with the advent of the turnpike roads. In the South Pennines short-haul gangs carried lime and coal up to the late nineteenth century, following the old roads over the hills rather than the new roads in the valleys, while single packhorses continued to be used until the 1940s for delivering bread and milk to upland farms.

Sue Hogg

Chapter 1 The Terrain

To understand the way of packhorse tracks it is necessary to rid the mind of all concepts of modern transport. The newcomer to the study of packhorse routes is at first amazed and bewildered by their apparently illogical meandering. He may find himself wandering north when his destination is to the south. So indoctrinated are we by the civil-engineering skills started by the canals and railways from 1650 onwards to our modern motorways, that we believe, just like the Romans, that the best and easiest route from A to B is a straight line. Consequently we have to visualize the topography of the countryside as it was in Britain prior to 1650.

The only through roads were the so-called King's Highways, but these were in so primitive a state that many of them could only be negotiated in summer. Britain north of a line drawn from Bristol to the Wash was a wilderness, known as *Britannia Inferior*, with scarcely a single bridge over the many rivers, except in the principal cities and market towns. Rivers were not navigable and the few roads for ox wains were only usable in summer. Conditions for travel were so bad that even the aristocracy only used their carriages in and around the towns. All cross-country travel was on horseback or a perilous adventure with a retinue of servants to pioneer a passage. Yet the country was alive with commerce and enterprise. So we discover the

HARD FOOTING ON THE SALTERGATE ABOVE TODMORDEN WITH STOODLEY PIKE ON THE SKYLINE

surprising fact that, prior to 1650, in *Britannia Inferior* all goods were transported by packhorse trains along well-defined routes which had been prospected over the wilderness by use over hundreds of years. And

THE MAIN ROUTE FROM ROCHDALE TO HALIFAX CROSSED THE WALSDEN VALLEY AT THE WATERSHED AND THEN CLIMBED TO SALTER RAKE END

now, after their decline, accelerated from 1850 onwards by the coming of the railways, we will come across sections of these well-worn trails today. It is the purpose of this book to describe features seen along these routes by which we can know for certain that here in days gone by was an artery of commerce equivalent to the railways of the nineteenth century and the motorways of the twentieth.

The slower the transport the greater the number of routes required; it was time-consuming to keep to the trunk routes, so more direct byways were improvised leading to every destination. Consequently, over the centuries a veritable spider's web of tracks was beaten out. Thus a study is not frustrated by the paucity but rather is confused by their great number and complexity. Every farm, every hamlet, every mine, quarry, corn mill, indeed, every establishment for whatever use had to have its packhorse track. The difficulty then is to limit one's investigation, to recognize which are purely local or for one specific purpose, such as carrying ore from a specific mine, and which are the through routes, the main highways for transporting general merchandise, named in parish records as 'pack and prime ways'.

In a mountainous region such as the Pennines, it might appear obvious that the valleys were the ideal routes for transport. This is indeed true for our comparatively modern canals, railways and motor roads, but it most definitely did not apply to the packhorse era. Just as a boat requires navigable water, the railway train iron rails and motor transport smooth highways, the packhorse required a through route of firm footing for the four slender legs that carried the burden. This criterion was not present in

WHEN THE CLIVIGER GORGE WAS A SWAMP THE
PACKHORSE TRACKS FROM BURNLEY RAN ALONG THE
HEIGHT. HERDERS' RAKE IS THE NARROW TRACK ON
THE RIGHT-HAND SIDE

the valleys before civil engineers such as Telford and
McAdam wrought considerable works.

The difficulty for packhorse transport was created by
the large number of small streams that poured down
from the uplands and into the valleys, where they
either gouged out formidable ravines or meandered
across the flat valley floor creating wide areas of
bogland. Before these streams were bridged by man
and the marshes drained, no packman dare risk his
team to a journey through the valleys. He had to seek
firm ground in the uplands and to ford the streams in
their infancy, or even go round their upper
extremities. This fact accounts for the apparently
illogical direction and tortuous routes taken by
packhorse tracks.

That is the reason why today we can still find many
packhorse tracks on our deserted uplands, and so
proceed with our intriguing discoveries into regimes
which flourished then disappeared over two hundred
years ago.

When the Norman overlords wished to travel
between their estates that William the Conqueror had
shrewdly scattered over his kingdom so as to prevent a
concentration of military power in one place, they
carried all their household and its effects with them
from castle to castle. They found the through roads to
be in such an execrable condition that they sent
instructions ahead for their fiefholders in each district
to be responsible for safe negotiation of their territory.

But the matter was even more serious when the king
himself wished to journey along the King's Highways
throughout his realm. The royal power endeavoured at
last to ensure a national system of trunk roads by an
Act of Philip and Mary in 1555, making each parish

ARTIST'S IMPRESSION OF THE GORGE IN THE
PACKHORSE ERA BY ROBERT WATSON

NAZE ROAD ABOVE THE WALSDEN VALLEY

responsible for the upkeep of its highways by stipulating that every able-bodied man was to freely give four days yearly of his labour with all necessary equipment for the upkeep of the King's Highway under the supervision of a 'voluntary' surveyor who was appointed on an annual basis. Unfortunately, because of difficulties of organization within the parishes, this Act did not have the desired effect, and even after the appointment of an honorary surveyor of highways and the imposition of a local rate, the national roads were still fraught with peril in summer and impassable in winter.

The year 1650 is chosen as a dividing line because the precursors of the turnpike roads were the justices' trusts (1663-1706), for which Parliament granted power to chief justices to adopt certain lengths of road, erect gates, and to collect tolls to cover the expenditure, particularly on continued maintenance. But the great breakthrough came in 1706 with the setting up of trusts, soon to be called turnpike trusts, in which a consortium of gentlemen was sanctioned to raise capital to build and maintain entirely new roads, so initiating the 'Turnpike Mania', following upon the 'Canal Mania' and only giving way to the 'Railway Mania' of the 1850s.

It is now possible to give a series of dates which were crucial to land transport in Britain:

1531: The Statute of Bridges gave justices the right to levy a county rate to cover costs of county bridges and to replace the old wooden bridges with stone ones

1555: Philip and Mary's Statute for repair of the King's Highway under the supervision of voluntary surveyors of highways by four days' work

1563: Elizabeth's Statute extending the number of days to six

1662: The first Act authorizing a highway rate

1663: Parliament's sanction for erection of gates and collection of tolls to maintain certain lengths of trunk road

1697: Justices authorized to erect guideposts at crossroads to nearest market town

1706: The first turnpike trust for building entirely new roads usually between market towns

1830: The first public railway

1875: Abolition and winding up of turnpike trusts

1894: Setting up of rural district councils under a county council with responsibility for local roads

Although not relevant to packhorse transport, to complete the series into modern times:

1921: Inauguration of a Ministry of Transport to take over the trunk roads and to develop dust-free road surfaces for motor vehicles, which had taken over from horsedrawn, and to pioneer traffic control with traffic lights, white lines, cat's eyes, roundabouts and pedestrian crossings, etc.

From the 1960s exclusive motorways were built, the road network having taken over from the railways for both passengers and goods.

What effect did all these regulations and new developments have on packhorse transport? The brief answer is: surprisingly little. Packhorse routes had evolved over a thousand years, ever since man had domesticated the horse. The spider's web of routes was essential to collect from and supply goods to isolated farms, villages and hamlets in an essentially agricultural environment. So life just went on regardless of government legislation.

It may be thought that the packhorse trains would flock onto the new turnpike roads for rapid and easy wayfaring, but this was not so for several reasons.

The food which powered the trains of some twenty to thirty animals was grass. The economics of the packhorse trade was so finely tuned for what was basically a very expensive mode of transport that the packman relied upon free grazing over the wastes, a facility not possible in the confines of a turnpike road. Economics again meant that the service could not afford the additional tolls, so much so that where the new turnpike was routed along an existing trail, new packhorse tracks were evolved to provide an alternative toll-free passage. This was particularly so where landowner members of a trust had blocked off ancient routes in an endeavour to force the pack trains onto their toll roads. Examples of packhorse bridges blanked off by huge stones can still be seen today.

Overnight stopping places had been long established, each with its own 'horse pasture'. There were no equivalent facilities on the turnpikes. Here the main provision was relatively expensive posting stations and inns to cater for a rapidly developing stagecoach system of passenger transport. Packhorse trains did not marry well with the speed and bustle of this innovation.

But the principal reason for the continued use of the ancient tracks was that, although the turnpike provided much improved communication between centres of commerce, the raw materials had still to be collected from, and finished goods delivered to, a widely scattered agricultural countryside. Turnpikes may have become the arteries, but the packhorse tracks were still the veins.

However, the packhorse establishment did benefit indirectly from the turnpike era. So long as these new roads were maintained from the tolls, the parish councils were happy to spend the highway rate, and use the statute labour, to improve the 'pack and prime ways' which were so vital to the welfare of the inhabitants.

Thus, evidence can still be found, on the ground, of considerable works of improvement obviously supervised by the parish surveyor. Sadly, some of these improvements, many dating from after 1750, came too late. I have found magnificent lengths of causeway stones that show no sign of wear and must have been little used in competition with the turnpikes, the canal

barges and then the railways with their delivery adjuncts of covered wagons, spelling the demise of packhorse transport after 1850.

I would like to record here that I rely upon a series of mid-century dates to record transport trends:

1550: The Statute of Philip and Mary, which laid the foundations for the development of a nationwide network of highways

1650: The beginning of the turnpike era

1750: The great expansion of trade routes due to the Industrial Revolution

1850: The railway age.

But, to return to our subject, in the great days of packhorse transport a typical journey would be as follows. Within the township there would be highways and byways connecting the farms to the corn mill, the fulling mill, the village green and church, and also lanes radiating outwards to moor gates leading onto the wastes both for the convenience of the parishioners and for travellers either coming or going. The packman would take the lane, often named after his destination, to pass through the township to his chosen moor gate. Within the farmlands his lane would, more often than not, be inclosed by good stone walls. For narrowgates these might only be 5 or 6 feet apart, for broadgates some 15 feet, and if the route was also a drove road it would be as wide as 33 or 44 feet. Because of the innate curiosity of farm animals, the villagers would have ensured that these lanes were stockproof and furnished with adequate field gates. Consequently, his team should have an easy passage through the inclosures of the township. Subsequent inclosures of the wastelands would have taken the final moor gate farther and farther out onto the moors and the nature of the lane and its walls would alter with each extension of the route. Happily, these township lanes would have been confirmed by use and by the inclosure awards as public rights of way. Unfortunately some of them may have been blocked off, quite illegally, but as this loss of use may have gone unchallenged for maybe a hundred years, and if they have not been correctly designated on the modern definitive map, it becomes a very lengthy and involved process to re-establish their rightful status.

Once through the moor gate the train was faced with all the hazards of high moors. Legally, before the inclosures, they had a right of way for any purpose in any direction. But in fact the packhorses would follow a well-beaten track developed over some three hundred to five hundred years to find firm footing for the diminutive hooves of the ponies. The hazards could vary from mountain torrents to deep ravines, peat bogs, 'clunters' of tussock grass or boulder-strewn outcrops. A rough rule was the cavalry man's dictum: 'Where rushes grow a horse can go.' But even this principle had to be applied with care for heavily laden animals.

As a result of these hazards the route would wander off in almost any direction to take the team round the tops of ravines or the sources of streams to find a ridgeway or a pass through the hills. Once established, the route was then subject to severe erosion, often manifest by deep holloways, but over the centuries man had fortified the vulnerable stretches with causeway pavements, artificial fords and even stone-built bridges to ease the way and avoid even longer detours.

ISSUES ROAD WEST OF HOLME. THIS BEAUTIFUL EXAMPLE OF A MOOR-GATE ROAD WAS SET OUT AS A PRIVATE CARRIAGE ROAD IN THE INCLOSURE. IT CONTINUES AS AN UNFENCED TRACK TO WESSENDEN HEAD

Also along the way, in passing from one parish to another or through small isolated settlements, there would be gateways flanked by great millstone grit posts with slots chiselled in to take a series of cross bars or 'stang poles'. The packman had to get his team through these without allowing the curious herds of summering cattle or ponies to follow him. At last he would arrive at the moor gate into the next set of inclosures, and once again negotiate a broadgate or narrowgate to his destination.

Such were the journeys of the regular traders along the so-called limersgates or saltways, but a horde of other carriers, chapmen and badgers would go off on side routes in almost any direction. In fact, the whole problem in the study of packhorse trails is their multiplicity. Unlike the turnpikes, which were few and finite in comparison and for which there are now well-documented records in public libraries, the walker or rider has to discover the pack routes for himself.

The student of the packways may well become discouraged, being bewildered by a network of seemingly infinite complication. There is only one way out of that, and that is to choose a distinctive trunk route such as a limersgate or a saltway. Even then the distractions of side tracks can lead to dead ends and frustration.

I myself have achieved the greatest satisfaction from chosing a specific point about which there can be no argument and tracing the routes from there. This is not always possible, however. For example, the Allescholes milestone appears to be at the dividing point of four important trade routes. This small block of millstone grit, high up on the bleak brink-edge of Reddyshore Scout above the Walsden valley, is inscribed: 'Burnley 9 miles Rochdale 5 miles Halifax 10 miles Todmorden 2 miles'. Identifying the routes is fraught with difficulties as one becomes bewildered by alternative ways over the rugged hills and valleys of the South Pennines. Even the 2-mile stretch to Todmorden is problematical, and as one wanders up hill and down dale one wonders whether the distances given on the stone are not statute miles but Yorkshire miles.

However, no attempt is to be made in this book to trace specific routes. Rather, the purpose is to describe features, man-made or otherwise, which are seen on the packhorse tracks and which are common to these tracks throughout the British Isles. My purpose is to enable the wanderer over the uplands to recognize them for what they are and know that he or she is indeed walking along an authentic packhorse way.

Chapter 2 Packhorse Bridges

It is our good fortune that the packhorse bridges were built of enduring materials, for no other feature has so captured the public imagination. They are even marked on the Ordnance Survey maps. We owe it to the appeal that these stone-built bridges have for the public that, although their commercial use died out nearly 200 years ago, interest in the packhorse tracks has never waned. On the contrary, it has become more positive as the years go by, so that today enthusiasts are not only tracing out and cataloguing these routes but endeavouring wherever possible to have them reinstated as bridleways.

The most popular bridge is, of course, the stone arch, of which interest is alike shared between fine many-arched structures over the main rivers and the little single-arched rough stone structures over the mountain streams.

In addition to arched bridges, there are many clapper bridges of huge flags laid across supporting pillars, clam bridges of massive slabs of rock balanced on pillars or thrown across gorges, and also cleverly constructed cantilever cross-overs. Each type deserves its own explanation.

Arched bridges

The stone arch, if held between immovable abutments, is virtually indestructible and is capable of carrying enormous weights way beyond the limits of ordinary use. It is difficult to imagine the load which would cause a stone arch to collapse, for it would have to be such as to literally crush the stonework into powder. Dare I say, no such load could be concentrated onto a packhorse bridge. Consequently they are indestructible and, if left alone, will endure for ever. This, as well as their beauty, is what endears them to the public. As the years have gone by it is almost as though they have grown, as part of a natural process, into their situation and, being of local materials, they enhance the picturesque scene of the landscape, in contrast to today's concrete horrors. Today people get out of their cars to look at packhorse bridges; they have become a tourist attraction.

The indestructibility which I have inferred only relates to their normal use as a load-carrying bridge, i.e. to downward forces in a vertical direction. The arched bridge is vulnerable to horizontal, sideways forces such as may occur in an abnormal flood or should the bridge aperture be blocked by an uprooted tree or by sudden releases of pack ice which have occurred over the centuries. Many hundreds of my 'indestructible bridges' have been swept away by floodwater exerting pressure upon them against which no provision had been made in their design.

Narrowness is the criterion by which a bridge can be assigned to packhorse days. Extreme narrowness for

BRIDGE OVER INGS BECK ON THE MONKS' WAY BETWEEN WHALLEY AND SAWLEY ABBEYS

sure-footedness and balance of the heavily laden beasts which crossed them without fear or question.

It is possible that many of the substantial parapets found today were added for the safety of pedestrians after the decline of packhorse use. They can be seen as obvious additions of fine slab-sided stonework reinforced and cleated together by wrought ironwork.

Some narrow bridges have been successively widened to suit the increase in road transport. It is a tribute to the strength of these stone arches that, although built three or four hundred years ago, they are still incorporated into modern arterial road bridges and daily carry burdens undreamed of by the original builders. Evidence of this progressive widening can clearly be seen from beneath and the portion of the original packhorse bridge identified.

There are two types of arched bridges: the 'humpbacked' or 'hog's back' and the 'straight-across'. The humpbacked is found where a stream or river passes through reasonably level country so that the arch has to rear up from the low level of the river banks. Such a bridge presents an arduous and

economy of building is responsible for a complete lack of parapets. Some authorities go to the length of asserting that only bridges without parapets are genuine pack bridges. They argue that parapets on narrow bridges would interfere with the smooth passage of the panniers on the ponies' backs. Yet many obviously authentic packhorse bridges have substantial parapets, and how thankful pedestrians are for these. The negotiation of bare humpback bridges can be quite dangerous and one can only marvel at the sometimes frightening task of climbing steeply up one arc to attain the summit and then the equally perilous descent down the opposing half. Again, one marvels at the agility and docility of a string of ponies which would unhesitatingly follow the leader over so formidable an obstacle, particularly if there was no reassuring parapet to hide the fearful drop into the water below. One such example is on the old monks' way between Whalley and Sawley abbeys over the Ings Beck near Chatburn, just below the viaduct on the Clitheroe to Hellifield railway line.

Many of these humpbacked bridges are so slender that the arch stones, including the all-important keystone, also perform the function of cobblestones for the horses' hooves. Notable examples are the picturesque Lumb Falls bridge and the double-arched bridge at Wycoller, which is much painted and photographed. It is possible to recognize the top surface of the archstones whilst walking over, giving the impression of a fragile structure of little solidity. However, so long as these stones remain in their true position, the slender arches have all the strength inherent in such a design.

Some humpbacks are named 'saddle bridges'. These rear up over a narrow rivulet and, having stone

parapets, they have the appearance of the wooden packsaddle used to distribute the load over the horse's back. The best-known one in Lancashire takes an important route from Whitewell/Bowland to Clitheroe over the Bashall Brook. It is lost in lovely countryside midway between Waddington and Browsholme Hall. David Hey writes of saddle bridges in Derbyshire.

The straight-across is contrived by building a bridge between the high banks of a stream which is flowing through a mini-ravine or gorge, and also by reducing the depth of the arch. The access routes are then high up, level with the top of the arch, and, by providing stonework upwards above the two halves of the arch,

SADDLE BRIDGE OVER THE BASHALL BROOK, NEAR BASHALL EAVES

a level track can be laid across the full length of the bridge, such as could not be done over a humpback. Consequently the straight-across bridges were ripe for upgrading by doubling their width into carriageways. Many of these are now incorporated into our present-day macadam byroads.

The portion built up above the arch to create a more or less level roadway was not merely composed of rubble held in place by dry-stone side walls, but was an architecturally constructed feature with consolidated ribs which transmitted the strength of the arch up to the load-bearing surface. These ribs are known as spandrels and were necessary not only to carry the weight but to prevent the vibrations set up by a packhorse team from loosening the structure so causing failure of these built-up features of the bridge. It is significant that troops of soldiers on the march were ordered to break step so as not to cause a dangerous vibration as they crossed a bridge. But one could not expect a team of trotting follow-my-leader horses to do likewise. Spandrels are almost as vital a component of a straight-across bridge as the basic arch, but unfortunately they are nearly always completely out of sight and therefore not appreciated.

In the hills, at the upper reaches of rivulets, many of the original narrow packhorse bridges remain. These were built to avoid taking the track even higher to skirt the source of the stream. In this way the journey was shortened and much rough going avoided.

Prior to the eighteenth century such bridges were built of rough stone, the naturally gifted eye of the dry-stone waller enabling him to select just the right size and

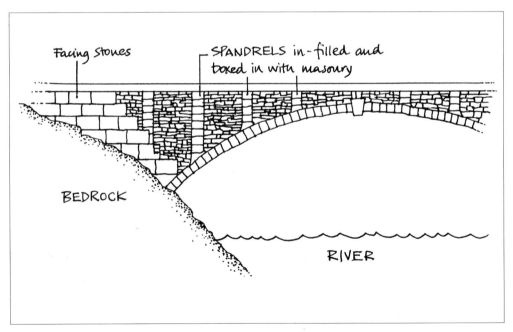

(above) THE FUNCTION OF SPANDRELS WAS TO SUPPORT THE ROADWAY

(opposite) CIRCULAR BRIDGE, PAUL CLOUGH, ON THE LANCASHIRE–YORKSHIRE BORDER

shape of stone to build an arch over a wooden frame and then secure the structure by driving in cleverly selected keystones at the top of the arch. He could then complete the bridge by the same technique as drystone walling. Such bridges were built at a minimum cost by local farmers, who had acquired the skills in their day-to-day work around the farm.

These bridges, made from undressed stone, are more picturesque and artistic than the precise and formal structures in which all the facing stones have been dressed by the mason's chisel.

However, from about 1750 onwards, with the opening of specialized quarries to provide stone to erect the mills of the Industrial Revolution, only dressed stone was acceptable to the bridge-builders. These men erected many graceful arches over our rivers and streams, but I repeat, these bridges are not as artistic as their natural rough-stone predecessors.

The majority of arches are shaped as an arc of a true circle. Indeed, it may be said that those encompassing a complete semicircle are Norman arches and were no doubt in the beginning conceived

by the Continental castle-builders.

However, with a shallow bridge it was not possible to accommodate a full semicircle so a smaller arc of a circle had to suffice. These are known as segmented arches, being a segment of a semicircle. The drawback of these was that they imposed a considerable side-thrust upon the abutments, which consequently had to be of immense strength to avoid complete failure of the arch. For multi-arched bridges the side-thrusts on the mid-river piers tend to cancel one another out and so present no problem.

There is one unusual bridge in Paul Clough, Cornholme, which is a complete circle with the stream running over the bottom arc. However, this bridge has no abutments and relies for its strength upon being consolidated by a considerable embankment, so that the packhorse track is on the top of this. This is more in the nature of a culvert than a bridge (see Chapter 3).

Although very rare, an occasional bridge may be found with a pointed arch. This may have been due to the need to raise the track higher above the water than

(above) BAKEWELL BRIDGE IN DERBYSHIRE

(left) CROMWELL'S BRIDGE OVER THE HODDER ON THE OLD PACKHORSE ROAD FROM PRESTON TO CLITHEROE

would have been possible with a Norman arch. Such arches are in the Gothic style of achitecture, and the most famous example is the splended five-arched Bakewell Bridge over the Wye in Derbyshire. Being now some six hundred years old, it must have been constructed by those superb craftsmen who built the abbeys and cathedrals of those days.

Not all the narrow stone arched bridges found in the countryside are packhorse bridges. To determine their use it is wise to investigate whether they are on a proven packhorse route. For example, Foster Bridge over the Hebden Water as this river approaches the town of Hebden Bridge appears to be a wonderfully preserved packhorse bridge. Investigation reveals that the approach to it is by a long flight of pedestrian steps with iron handrails coming down from the environs of Heptonstall, while its other end terminated in the mill yard of the huge Foster cotton mill, now a housing estate with only the stump of the great mill chimney remaining. Foster Bridge was, then, a footbridge, built by the mill owner so that his workers could have easy access to the mill when in the winter months their comings and goings were in total darkness. Shedden Bridge, near Hurstwood, has also been described as a packhorse bridge, but is in fact an estate bridge, not built until 1906 for Sir John Thursby of Ormerod Hall to give access to his shooting estate based on Shedden Farm.

Another apparently perfect packhorse bridge at Beckfoot Mill, near Bingley, was a footbridge for the workers. The genuine Beckfoot bridge is some hundred yards lower down the Harden Brook, a lovely humpback alongside the ford at Beckfoot Farm. The

(above) THE SMALLEST BRIDGE I KNOW – AT THE TOP OF HIPPINS CLOUGH, BLACKSHAW HEAD

(right) OS FIRST EDITION 6-INCH MAP SHOWING HARLEY WOOD GATE AND HIPPINS CLOUGH, BLACKSHAW HEAD

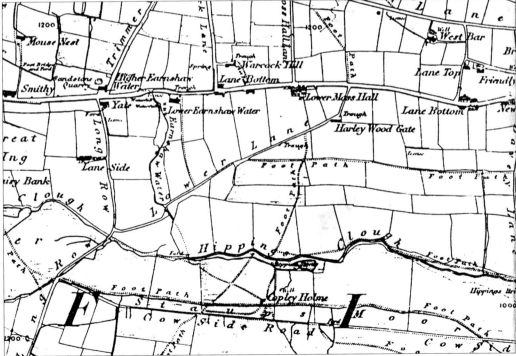

horses would certainly have used the bridge when the river was in spate.

Most of the bridges I have referred to are single-arch, but, of course, they can have any number of arches to span the river's width. However, I cannot recall any example with more than four arches in the South Pennines. The magnificent stone bridge which has given its name to the town of Hebden Bridge has thankfully been preserved in its original state since it replaced an earlier wooden bridge in 1510 AD. For nearly 350 years pack trains coming down the Buttress from Heptonstall crossed over the Hebden Water here before climbing up the Snicket to Midgley on the busy clothiers' route between Burnley and Halifax.

The graceful three-arched Lower Hodder packhorse bridge on the track from Preston to Clitheroe, though no longer in use even as a footpath, is thankfully preserved. Named Cromwell's Bridge, it suggests a study of the military use of packhorse bridges throughout our turbulent history may be fruitful. The infamous bridge at Bannockburn springs readily to mind, with decisive battles at Boroughbridge and Stamford Bridge, and the bridge that was broken down over the Don, remembered in the naming of Pontefract.

A feature of long, multi-arched bridges is the refuges for pedestrians caught on a bridge as a train with wide pannier bags comes clattering over. These are contrived from the V-shaped cutwaters of the mid-stream abutments rising vertically up to V-shaped parapets on the trackway. There are cutwaters on both sides, the downstream ones preventing cavitation from undermining the piers.

The longest packhorse bridge in England is at Great Haywood in Staffordshire, the only one over the River Trent. There are fourteen arches and each of the thirteen piers has cutwaters on either side, with a total of twenty-six refuges along the 100-yard length.

Of two-arched bridges, perhaps the artist's favourite is the quaint medieval pack bridge at Wycoller, near Colne.

To illustrate the infinite variety of these bridges, a curiosity is the tiny but perfectly made arched bridge over the stream at the very top of Hippins Clough, near Blackshaw Head. This miniature, of course, has no parapets, is only 55 inches between the abutments, 26 inches above the water, and 60 inches wide, yet it appears to have had considerable use. It is on a track known as the Harley Wood Gate, which essentially is part of the route from Shore-in-Stansfield to Heptonstall. To find it, follow the causeway stones up from Hippins Bridge to the northwest corner of that peculiar patch of ground called Staups Moor.

Clapper bridges

Contemporary writers lead us to believe that packhorse trains were kept going at a fair pace, and the sound of such a team clattering over a flagged bridge accounts for the name 'clapper'.

Such bridges are made of very strong flagstones supported by pillars rising from the bed of the stream. For stability the flags have to be laid perfectly level, so a clapper bridge is a true 'straight-across'. Hence the speed with which it could be negotiated. This 'straight-across' feature also means that such a bridge has to be located where the stream banks are some 3 to 5 feet above the water level.

They are narrow bridges, being only the width of a single flagstone, and are never provided with parapets,

THE AUTHOR ON THE CLAPPER BRIDGE, MALHAM

although iron handrails might have been fitted when they no longer took the wide packs of the ponies and were then used as footbridges only. The flagstones were subject to considerable wear by the iron-shod hooves, so that a deep groove was worn down the centre. Stones were sometimes dressed to remove this ankle-straining problem or a fresh surface was provided by turning the flags over. However, this groove could weaken the stone to the point of breakage, hence clapper bridges are nowhere near as reliable and enduring as arched bridges.

One of the best-known clappers is again at Wycoller and here one of the spans was broken during repair work, so an additional pillar had to be built beneath the break line.

Clapper bridges can have any number of spans, particularly when passing over wide shallow streams with gravelly or rocky beds. So why provide a bridge over what would appear to be an ideal ford? The answer is that, in spate, a depth of over, say, 12 inches would build up against the low-slung panniers and sweep a light pony off its feet. There was also the need to keep the saleable goods in the packs free from water damage or there would be no payment for the carriage.

Clam or slab bridges

A clam bridge consists of a huge slab of sandstone or millstone grit flung across a stream, usually where it courses in a mini-ravine between rocky banks. 'Clam' has the same meaning as 'clamp'. The great slab of stone is secured, or clamped, in position possibly in a groove chiselled in the bedrock, or perhaps held firm by surrounding stonework mortared in. In this way the slab is locked and immovable under the onslaught of a packhorse train and, just like the small rough-stone arch bridges, appears to be part of the landscape. It enhances rather than detracts from the view.

Most slab bridges are a single stone over a raging mountain brook, such as the one below Beverley Banks in Jumble Hole Clough on a minor pack route from East Lee to the Heptonstall Cloth Hall.

My favourite is the Hebble Hole bridge in the lower Colden valley. This took the old Long Causeway from Burnley to Halifax over the Colden Water before Jack Bridge was built. It consists of two halves resting on a huge boulder in the middle of the stream, each half comprising two massive slabs arranged side by side, so that there are four remarkably evenly matched slabs in all. At some time in the last century this bridge was blocked off by a stone post placed in the centre of the bridge on the Blackshaw Head side of the stream. This was possibly done to force traffic onto the Burnley-Halifax turnpike road, or the old route may have been diverted via Jack Bridge.

One marvels at how local people transported these great stones and placed them in position, each weighing many tons. I can only presume that they moved them on sledges pulled by a team of heavy

CLAM BRIDGE ACROSS JUMBLE HOLE CLOUGH JUST BELOW STAUPS MILL

HEBBLE HOLE BRIDGE OVER COLDEN WATER

Stonework of natural rock is fashioned to rise some 4 or 5 feet above the water, one on either side. The top surface of these plinths is given a slight down-throw from the water edge so that a flagstone on each one, tilted slightly upwards, can be projected for a short distance over the stream.

So we then have two protrusions facing each other on either side, with a considerable gap in between. When these are counterbalanced by heavy flagstones placed on their inboard ends they become the cantilevers, on which a long flagstone is placed to bridge the gap. This centre stone will carry quite heavy loads, of course depending upon the weight of the counterbalancers. However, we now have an irregular sequence of stones for the packhorse to negotiate, especially an awkward step up from the cantilevers onto the centre span. This problem is solved by laying a surface of flags over the structure to give a smooth walkway across the bridge. The top layer may hide the true load-bearing cantilevers, so confusing a true understanding of the mechanics, which can only be ascertained from below.

horses, then manœuvred them on wooden rollers and, using tcchniqucs learned from the seamen, lifted them into position by ropes and pulleys suspended from improvised shearlegs.

Cantilever bridges

The best-known example of a cantilever bridge is the Firth of Forth railway bridge, a truly epic structure of world renown. However, infinitely smaller packhorse bridges rely on exactly the same principle to carry heavy loads across a stream without the need for a central pillar.

There is a delightful sketch of the cantilever bridge adjacent to the Brontë Waterfall, some 2 miles from Haworth, in Whiteley Turner's book *A Springtime Saunter*. Thankfully this is a very clear representation of the bridge before it was swept away by the disastrous flood of 1984, when much of the original stonework was lost. The bridge has since been rebuilt

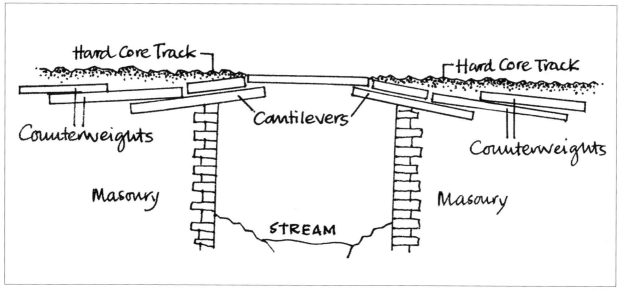

(above) CANTILEVER BRIDGE

(below) THE PREHISTORIC CANTILEVER BRIDGE IN NEWSHOLME DEAN – THIS EXAMPLE IS A FOOTBRIDGE

to its original design using demolition flags from cotton mills and this alien stone has not yet weathered sufficiently to hide the fact that it is not the original bridge.

Although not part of a bridge's structure, the bed of the stream was often paved to facilitate an even flow of water and to prevent erosion undermining the all-important abutments. Also, an apron was sometimes provided upstream to collect the water for safe and rapid transit. This would prevent the build-up of debris against the face of the bridge and even in times of flood guide such dangerous objects as tree trunks safely through.

Another common feature is the use of water gates to prevent animals from straying under the bridge; these were hinged to prevent a build-up of trash.

Chapter 3 Culverts and Fords

Apart from bridges, there are two other devices for crossing the many streams that run down from the high moors: culverts and fords.

Culverts

A culvert is a conduit for carrying a flow of water underground for a considerable distance. Where a deep ravine crossed the most convenient route, the packhorse trail would have to make a tedious detour to the head of the stream to circumvent the ravine. To obviate this, and so shorten the length and severity of the route, a culvert was constructed along the bed of the stream to carry the flow of water, and then covered by an earthen embankment. This was consolidated across the ravine and surfaced with either hardcore or a pavement, or both. Earth embankments have to be built at a certain angle to achieve soil stability, as can be seen in the construction of reservoir dams. This means that if the top is to be, say, 10 feet wide, the bottom will be several times this width depending on the depth of the ravine. The culvert must therefore be of considerable length to accommodate the embankment, but also must be large enough to take any foreseeable flood water.

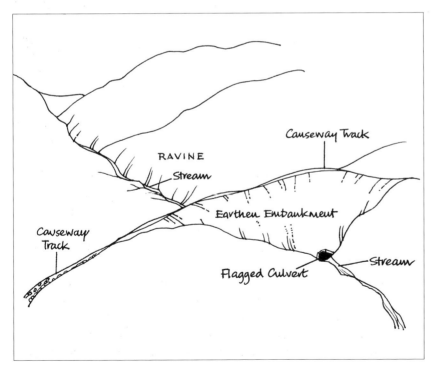

RAVINE

Stream

Causeway Track

Causeway Track

Earthen Embankment

Flagged Culvert

Stream

CAUSEWAY OVER CULVERTED
STREAM AND EMBANKMENT

The era in which these culverts were constructed was before industry had learned the techniques of making large-diameter pipes in earthenware, concrete or plastic; nor was Portland cement in common use. Consequently many culverts were stone-arched all the way through, and smaller ones were of a square section constructed from flag-stones. Beneath high embank-ments the culvert was often a complete stone-encased circle for strength. Where stone was scarce I have found culverts of early brickwork. Indeed, exploring culverts bent almost double and carrying a shaded candle – because there was invariably a draught – was a foolhardy phase of my boyhood.

CULVERT ON THE OLD LONG CAUSEWAY AT STIPERDEN FARM

Over the past few hundred years these culverts and embankments have grown into the landscape, becoming covered with trees and shrubs, so that they may go unrecognized, like the one which takes the Earnshaw Water beneath the Long Causeway to the west of Blackshaw Head.

This latter also provides a clue as to who built these features, for its repair is mentioned in the Stansfield township records. It is reasonable to presume that these valuable improvements to packways were done by the township fulfilling its obligations first set out in Philip and Mary's Act of 1555, by which every farmer had to send his labourers and horse and carts to do four days' work each year to repair the roads leading between market towns. An embankment could be thrown up in a few days' intensive work. But of course the surveyor would first have constructed the culvert, using skilled men paid out of the highway rate.

Not all culverts are of necessity covered by high embankments. Across shallow streams a short culvert was often used instead of a conventional bridge, with a low embankment to consolidate the culvert in position. This would be no higher than a bridge, and carried the packhorse track straight across the stream. There are many of these culverts doing duty for a bridge, and I mention one in particular where I was certain there would be a rough stone-arched bridge.

This is where the old line of the Long Causeway passes from Lancashire into Yorkshire at Stiperden over what in older times was called the Crowbrook, and which is still the demarcation between the two counties.

Fords

The ford is the simplest way of crossing a river or brook. The large number of placenames ending in 'ford' gives a clear indication that originally there were hundreds of fords in the road system of the British Isles. And in the hills, crisscrossed by packhorse tracks, there were again hundreds of streams which could perhaps be crossed by fording. It was only necessary to check the depth of the water, and then splash your way across.

But, although the streambed and the flow of water may have been no problem, it was first of all necessary to enter and leave the streambed. In choosing a location for a ford, it was the suitability of the approaches, rather than the actual stream crossing, that was of paramount importance. Heavily laden animals had to have a smooth progression into and out of the water. The best location was where the stream ran over a wide ledge of the rock strata. Where the topography did not supply a natural ford with firm approaches, an artificial ford was often constructed. However, like so many other man-made features on the packhorse routes, these

artificial fords have weathered and merged into their surroundings. The trick was to build a very strong stone dam across the stream, and then, instead of allowing deep water to build up behind it on the upstream side, to fill the cavity right up to the sill of the dam with shingle. There were now two effects: the dam widened the stream and so reduced its depth; and the shingle consolidated itself and was constantly replenished by the stream to provide excellent footing for the packhorse trains.

Some of these dams may have only been token affairs with just a low wall to increase the width of the stream, but where there was a rocky gorge with a swift

METHOD OF CONSTRUCTION OF THE MAN-MADE FORD AT GILFORD CLOUGH, TRAWDEN

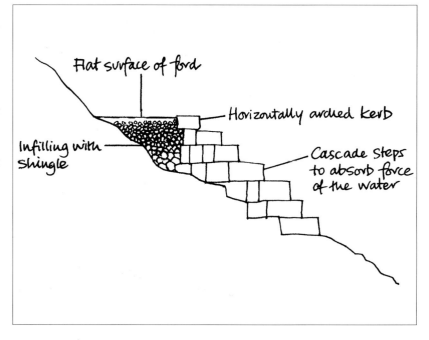

THE CASCADE AT GILFORD CLOUGH

'caul' after the high, curved head-dress worn by Elizabethan ladies.

The best example of such a caul that I know of is on a little-known track which was used to take the woollen pieces of the Trawden handloom weavers first along Boulsworth Bottom to the head of Thursden valley, then over Widdop to Heptonstall, and later to Halifax. The ford, with its shingle crossing and spectacular cascade down nine steps, is in Gilford Clough on the outskirts of upper Trawden. It is a gem that should be reconditioned and preserved.

While on the subject of fords, it is opportune to remark that the packhorse teamsters must have been students of the weather, because they had to know for certain that their train could reach its planned overnight resting place and not be caught out by high water levels after heavy rains. The modern haulier, if held up, can switch off his engine and go to sleep in his cab, but the teamster had flesh and blood in his care. It is more tiring to stand still bearing a heavy load than to walk with steady rhythm, so packsaddles would have to be lifted off, with measures to protect the merchandise from damage, some thirty or forty horses, a daunting task in an inhospitable location. Then the ponies had to be turned loose to graze or they would rapidly lose the stamina required for perhaps a long detour. To guard against such crises, there were always alternative routes; indeed, in many areas there were winter and summer tracks between the same destinations. It was the teamster's knowledge of the locality, of the weather and of the hazards that was crucial in his decision as to which route to take.

flow of water it was necessary to build a curved solid structure of kerbstones of considerable height, with the kerbs arranged in stepped courses down which the overflow cascaded. Such a curved cascade is named a

Chapter 4 The Causeways

As the trodden portion of a pioneer track became more and more treacherous, it was found necessary to delineate and fortify the route with a stone pavement, which then became known as a 'causey' or later a 'causeway'. The word 'causey' is derived from the Old French *cauci* meaning a 'raised or paved way', an apt description of a packhorse track.

Ideally the pavement was constructed from very strong rectangular flagstones with their long axis laid at right angles across the track. This ensured that the ponies placed their hooves on the centre of the stones, so distributing their considerably concentrated weight evenly onto the subsoil. Should the stones have been placed lengthways, which would have been far more economical in first cost, the danger would have been of the ponies putting their weight onto one end and so tilting or working loose the pavement, even producing rocking stones, which would have inhibited the confidence of the teams in striding boldly along the causeway. Causeways were very narrow, not more than a yard in width, the usual being from 24 to 27 inches. A statute of 1691 called for a minimum width of 3 feet.

However, although there are some fine stretches of evenly shaped flagstones, most causeways are paved with rough and ready boulders gleaned from the locality. As with drystone walling, the artisan selects a

AN EARLY CAUSEWAY – KENNEL LANE, OXENHOPE

LONG CAUSEWAY, LANGFIELD COMMON

area, resulting in a considerable groove caused by the iron-shod hooves.

The amount of use of particular routes can be gauged today by the depth of these grooves. However, well-used tracks may have had the stones replaced and one device was to turn over stones which had an alternative face. There is written evidence that regular maintenance was carried out on the 'pack and prime' causeys from the parish rate. However, a causeway was a very durable item and hundreds of miles, even though much is now buried beneath the top soil, remain for the enthusiast to explore.

It is generally believed that causeways were only laid on soft ground, such as peat, but most such have long since disappeared from human sight. The fine examples which are found today are invariably on good, firm ground.

In early times the nature of the countryside in the hills was described by its colour, as, particularly at certain times of the year, the landscape was a kaleidoscope of different colours. The prominent division was between black and white, although there were also green, brown and red. The areas were described by these colours, as, for example, Black Hameldon, Black Clough, White Hill, Whiteandale, Whitewell, and there were also Redmires, Brown Birks, Greenholes. Black land was invariably peatland varying in colour from jet black to russet brown. White land was predominantly clay with a dense cover of bent grass whose fragile seed heads reflected the

'face' to present to the public, and in the case of the causeway buries his boulder firmly into the trackway with the smooth face uppermost. He may even have trimmed the surface, and in some cases cross-furrowed it to avoid slipping, although some causeways became named as Slippery Stones.

It is surprising how many huge stones were pressed into service, and even stretches of bedrock were incorporated, and this is where a certain amount of trimming and scoring was called for. Again, as with the drystone waller, the workman uses his innately artistic eye in marrying a random selection of boulders into a presentable causeway.

The trackways so produced were not very wide, 27 inches being about the average width. Consequently the wear was concentrated upon a very small central

white light and at times glistened like silver. Red was from the seeding bog myrtle, sorrel or dock. Brown was brown bent, while green was sphagnum moss or patches of bracken or good pasture and meadowland.

The causeways over black land have disappeared, and the good examples remaining are on white land. This is land which can be reclaimed from the moor by draining and liming, and so it attracted much packhorse traffic for the reclamation work. The black land was of little agricultural value and certainly uneconomical to improve. It also presented a hazard which nevertheless had to be crossed, and causeway stones were the only answer.

But why were causeways built over good firm land? The most apparent reason would seem to be to prevent erosion, but I believe the aim was to present an even track for high-speed trunk routes, serving the same function as motorways today.

Continuous stretches of pavement on trunk routes are often named Long Causeway, and are still recorded on the Ordnance Survey maps. There are three of these not far from my locality. The best known is the Long Causeway running from Mereclough, near Burnley, to Blackshaw Head on the old packhorse track from Burnley to Halifax, which is now a motor road. This route was of such importance in the seventeenth and eighteenth centuries that a special clause was inserted in the Halifax-Burnley Turnpike Act of 1759 stipulating that no gates had to be placed across the ancient highway which ran to Burnley via Heptonstall, Blackshaw Head and Keb Cote. A second Long Causeway is the pavement from Lumbutts up and over Langfield Common to Withens and Cragg Vale, whilst a third – Ramsden

Long Causeway – climbs over Crook Moor from Watergrove near Wardle to Inchfield above Walsden.

Causeways run both on the level and up and down hill. Some of the routes are so steep that it is quite surprising that the ponies could climb up without slipping. One such is the above-mentioned Langfield Long Causeway over the height that is crowned by the

monument on Stoodley Pike. I should estimate that the maximum gradient for a continuous causeway is 1 in 8. Steeper than this and the stones had to be laid level and rise in steps to form what became known in packhorse days as a 'staircase'. I know of several of these but the only confirmed example is on the track from Heptonstall to Haworth where that portion of the route over Oxenhope Moor is named Top of Stairs on the Ordnance Survey maps, with a Stairs Hill, Stairs Edge, Stairs Bottom, Stairs Hole, Stairs Swamp and finally Stairs Lane. These names vividly indicate the nature of the wild moor negotiated by intrepid carriers. On this route many of the steps were improvised from the outcrop of sandstone ledges.

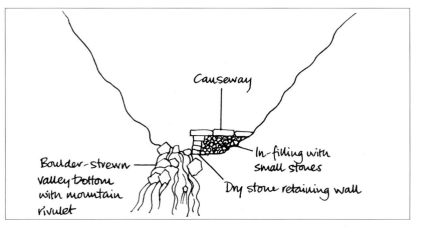

SHELFWAY CARRYING A CAUSEWAY DOWN A BOULDER-STREWN CLOUGH

ELEVATED CAUSEWAY ON SALTER RAKE GATE NEAR LUMBUTTS

On one of the limersgates running from the Craven limestone into the West Riding there is a stepped causeway known as Lumb Stairs. It climbs up from the lovely packhorse bridge and romantic beauty spot, Lumb Falls, to the old road from Hebden Bridge to Haworth, which the pack route crosses before traversing Cock Hill Moor into Luddenden Dean. However, this staircase has been repaired by the local authority and has lost much of its original character.

In a few instances where the traffic was heavy in both directions and the gradient was long and steep the route was made to zigzag down the hillside and the whole width was paved with small, beautifully tooled stone setts. One fine example is the descent from the Inchfield plateau down to a bridge over the Midgelden stream at Gauxholme on the track from Watergrove by way of Ramsden Long Causeway and Ragby Bridge. The section down to Gauxholme is known as Naze Road. This use of setts was a refinement of the stone causeway. It was found to be so successful in

SHELFWAY AT GRAINING WATER, WIDDOP

into a valley and back out again was on what was called a 'rake', i.e. a track running at a comparatively gentle angle across the slope of the hillside. There are innumerable such rakes marked on the Ordnance Survey maps, a good example being Salter Rake Gate, which climbs from North Hollingworth almost to the summit of Langfield Edge to round the knoll at Rake End, and then descends on another long rake down to the Shepherd's Rest and Lumbutts.

And this brings me to a feature found on causeways which goes generally unremarked but which is almost unbelievable for the amount of labour involved in its construction. This feature is a flat-topped mound elevated some 8-10 inches above the surrounding moor with the causeway stones firmly embedded in its top surface. These elevated causeways can only have been provided by carting and carefully placing thousands of loads of catt or clay. But that is not all. They were carefully drained with cross-dykes bridged by miniature stone-slab bridges. The Salter Rake track passes the Shepherd's Rest on such an elevated causeway.

One other type of built-up trackway for causey stones may be found alongside wild and rocky

providing a grip for the iron-shod hooves of working horses that it became the norm for all the roads and streets in the Lancashire cotton towns before the advent of the motor vehicle.

One of the vilest staircases must be the climb up the well-nigh precipitous valley side from the ford at Hebden Hey in Hardcastle Craggs to Slack Chapel. This zigzags upward with such rough steps that it would seem impossible for a packhorse train to negotiate them. Yet climb them they did, with full pack, following with instinctive obedience the indomitable leader, usually an old mare, which was the teamster's indispensable asset.

However, the easiest way to take a causeway down

mountain streams, where the valley floor is impossibly uneven and indented. An earthen shelf is constructed and consolidated along the brook side by a drystone retaining wall, giving a smooth and even bed for the causeway. A good example can be found in the remote and rocky gorge of the Graining Water where it diverges from the motor road in Widdop to join the Gorple stream.

This has been incorporated into the Pennine Way and the section of this route from Reaps to Widdop Road provides walkers with a variety of causeway features as it winds its way through two spectacular gorges. Unfortunately the packhorse bridge over the Widdop stream has been swept away, and has been replaced by a wooden footbridge. The Gorple stream is crossed by a ford on solid rock and the track then runs as a staircase rake out of the ravine up to Reaps Cross and the junction of several trails. The route is shown on the Heptonstall township map and on a Towneley estate map, both in Calderdale Archives.

Raised causeways may also be found at the side of cartways and old holloways (see Chapter 5). In these cases the laying of a causeway appears to have followed upon the clearing out of the holloway, probably to widen it into a cartway. The spoil was banked up on one side to enable it to dry out and to form a good hard ridge on which to lay the causeway stones. The packhorses then used the causeway, leaving the holloway for unshod cattle and carts.

Following upon the Turnpike Mania after 1750, work was sometimes put in hand to upgrade packhorse causeways from narrowgates to broadgates. This practice was particularly prevalent in the Rochdale area and was achieved by burying flat edging stones vertically on either side of the causey stones some 10 feet apart to form a kerb, and surfacing between the edging stones and the causey stones with hardcore. In this way the track could be used by carts and carriages with the horse walking on the central causeway and the vehicle's wheels on the hardcore. It is my belief that such a construction accounts for the so-called Roman Road down Blackstone Edge to Littleborough. Such upgraded routes largely failed because, unlike the turnpikes, they had not been engineered for wheeled transport. The gradients were too severe and routes themselves often involved tortuous and longer journeys.

One such is the above-mentioned Ramsden Long Causeway from Watergrove to Inchfield, upgraded in the 1830s and which I am convinced was never used because there is no sign of wear on the causeway stones. That is not to say that the original causeway was not used, only that the upgraded broad track with its refurbished pavement failed to attract traffic away from the much easier turnpike road through Calderbrook and Walsden.

Like bridges, causeways were of military significance. It is recorded that the people of Huddersfield and Holmfirth tore up 2,000 yards of causeway over the moor to discourage Bonny Prince Charlie from coming over from Lancashire into Yorkshire. Consequently he took the Derbyshire route for his attempted raid on London.

The narrowness of the single-track causeway led to considerable difficulties when teams met travelling in opposite directions. The confrontation could lead to violence, and it is believed that teamsters and their retinue carried strong staves, or even knobsticks, for

LOST CAUSEWAY ON HUDSON MOOR, STANSFIELD, EXCAVATED BY PENDLE ARCHAEOLOGICAL GROUP IN 1986

it must be recorded that in these circumstances reason prevailed and all hands rescued any bogged down animal.

In order to avoid these difficulties, a train proceeded with as much noise as possible. Each pony's saddle was fitted with an iron hoop from which bells were suspended giving a constant jingle, whilst the lead horse – known as the bell mare – wore a bell round its neck. In addition, when approaching a blind bend or a difficult part of the track the teamsters would shout out in warning.

Even single travellers came to grief on narrow causeways, particularly in the winter. In 1683 Oliver Heywood describes how, travelling from Northowram to Sowerby one winter's day, he gave a lift to a friend on the back of his horse. They narrowly escaped disaster when, 'passing to a place where my horse was loath to go on an yce, went on the causey, the upper way, but it was so narrow and near the wall that our knees and legs hitting the wall, justled the horse down into the lower way, yet fell not but light on its feet' (*Diaries*, IV, p. 102). The Leeds antiquarian Ralph Thoresby was not so lucky when, crossing Blackstone Edge in the snow in February 1698, his horse fell and crushed his leg.

When the packhorse trails fell into disuse, the causeway stones were rapidly overgrown by grass turves and after a few years completely disappeared from sight. Today there must be more lengths of causeway buried than those still visible. Long lengths have also disappeared beneath tarmacadam when the tracks were upgraded to motor roads. This presents a great problem in tracing the old line of true packhorse trails.

either offence or defence. Usually the strongest team asserted its right of way. Many times the displaced ponies were left floundering in soft ground, although

Chapter 5 Holloways and Ridgeways

Where the surface of a track is not protected by a causeway some erosion is bound to occur. When the ponies are restricted to a particular narrow track, depending upon the durability of the subsoil, the ensuing wear results in a holloway. Holloways are possibly the best indication of the use of a route as a packhorse track, and the depth of the holloway is a measure of the importance and age of that route as an arterial highway. Holloways are most significantly found today where the laden teams had to surmount hillsides.

Another phenomenon is a series of holloways side by side running parallel to each other up a hillside. This is because when the bottom of the first holloway became choked up with mud and debris, the teamster moved over to start a fresh one.

To produce a holloway two agents are required: water and mechanical abrasion. In the Pennines water was never scarce to soften the surface, and the breakdown of this surface inevitably followed the abrasion caused by hundreds of shod hooves. The flow of water down the narrow bottom of the holloway was then able to scour it out and so continuously increase its depth.

However, not all linear hollows down hillsides were gouged out by packhorses. Some are man-made hushings for extracting minerals from a metallized fault or glacial drift. The sod was first removed to make a furrow, down which a rush of water, previously impounded behind an earthen dam, was

KNOWN LOCALLY AS THE OLD SCOTCH ROAD, THIS HOLLOWAY ABOVE THE THURSDEN VALLEY LEADS ONTO BOULSWORTH HILL

BRIDGELEY BANK AND THE SERIES OF HOLLOWAYS ON THE STEEP ASCENT OF HAMELDON HILL

Series of corrugations on either side of a ridge were caused by meltwater from the last Ice Age scouring away the drift while it was still friable, just as the retreating tide leaves ripples in the sand. The hump of the Little End of Pendle is particularly noted for dozens of grooves on either side of the hill which could be mistaken for packhorse holloways, but which were in fact scoured out by the run-off from the melting ice.

Consequently, an indentation can only be described as a holloway if it is unmistakably on the line of an authenticated packhorse route.

directed. Men worked from the bottom of the furrow upwards, loosening the subsoil with mattocks and extracting the mineral-bearing pebbles. When the hushing was worked out, they moved on to begin a new one, thus eventually leaving a serrated landscape which could not be backfilled because all the overburden had been washed away into the main rivers and so out to sea. These serrations, called 'grooves', were worked by teams of men until all the surface deposits had been worked out. Then it became necessary to sink shafts, but in seventeenth-century lead mines these shafts were still called 'grooves'.

Some holloways running down a hillside were originally exploratory measures to discover new faults which could be mined. Other holloways can be found running from quarries; these were known as sled gates, sledges being used to bring out stone.

For examples of hillside holloways one can do no better than explore Dunnockshaw where, just past Bridgeley Bank, four parallel holloways, used alternatively by pack teams climbing steeply up to the plateau of Hameldon Hill, are plainly discernible. On the other side of the Burnley-Rawtenstall road the Limers' Lane climbs in an exceptionally deep holloway which curves round to circumvent the lost village of Gambleside on the track's way to the summit at Compston's Cross. This is part of a limers' way from Clitheroe to Rochdale and also on the ancient route from Burnley to Manchester via Cowpe and Rooley Moor Road. However, there are holloways by the hundred all over the countryside.

Holloways are not confined to hillsides, but can be found on the level where there is no causeway to protect the surface. Depending on the nature of the subsoil, such holloways can be worn down into trenches as deep as 20 feet. In these cases there is a problem of drainage, for the whole length could fill up with water in heavy rains. Advantage had to be taken of the slightest slope to drain the water away by a man-made ditch, called a 'grip', wherever this was possible. Even so, the track in the bottom is often filled with several inches of muddy water.

I have heard it argued that these holloways on level land were not worn down by the horses but were dug out with spades in an endeavour to find a firm bottom and so avoid laying a causeway. I believe that this is a half truth, for an old man, whose reminiscences came from generations back, told me that men used to be set on to clear the mud out periodically. Consequently, although the packhorses caused the initial erosion, the cleaning-out by statute labour accelerated the process.

LONDON'S HOLLOWAY IN 1776 (from M. J. Armstrong, *Great Post Roads between London and Edinburgh*)

DARK LANE, RODMER CLOUGH – A VERY ANCIENT HOLLOWAY PAVED WITH CAUSEWAY STONES

OX LEE LANE, HEPWORTH: CONSTRUCTED HOLLOWAY WITH A LARGE STONE DRAIN DOWN THE CENTRE

Barnet, through the districts of Highgate and Holloway to Islington. Once a distinct holloway through a rural landscape, it is now completely absorbed by the capital's built-up sprawl.

A ridgeway is the exact opposite of a holloway in almost every aspect. Having endured geologically and meteorologically for millions of years, its top surface is as hard as iron. A packhorse team struggles through the mud of a holloway in which it is lost to the world, but it strides easily and confidently along a ridgeway silhouetted against the skyline for all to see. Holloways are possibly the most numerous manifestations of the packhorse tracks, while ridgeways are comparatively rare. Holloways are easily recognized for what they are, but, because of its hard surface, a ridgeway shows little signs of use and is can only be counted as part of a trackway if other features indicate that it is on a recognized route.

The best known holloway in the public eye is the one notorious for its gaol. It was worn down over the centuries by the immense amount of traffic of every description pouring into London from the north. Much of the traffic would have been drovers' herds on the hoof, and even geese from Norfolk paddling along, but by far the greatest proportion would have been packhorse trains supplying the capital with all its land-borne merchandise. London's Holloway is a continuation of High Street running south from

A ridge is usually the high ground between two neighbouring rivers or streams, a symmetrical formation with a definite line or route along its summit from which the water runs away naturally down either side. This line being dry and bone-hard presents an ideal packhorse track, always providing it runs in the right direction.

Ridges are windswept and there are even times when the wind is so strong that a passage dare not be attempted. Here again a ridgeway is in direct contrast to a holloway. But the force and scouring action of the wind can be beneficial in clearing a ridge of all obstacles except the largest boulders.

Perhaps not as well known as the London Holloway, the historic Ridgeway is nevertheless a far more imposing feature, stretching as it does from Wiltshire along the brow of the Chiltern Hills as far as Bedfordshire. It was a prehistoric highway for the collection of flint from Grimes Graves in Norfolk.

Although these were not strictly packhorse tracks, I mention them to illustrate the continuity of such words over the centuries. Words were adopted from ancient times and some have passed into modern usage, indicating a smooth transition over the ages from one mode of transport to another.

There is another topological feature that is akin to a ridge, and that is an edge. This differs from a ridge in that there may be a plateau or gentle slope on one side

A SPECTACULAR EDGEWAY, REDDYSHORE SCOUT GATE ABOVE THE WALSDEN VALLEY

NAZE ROAD: FIRM FOOTING FOR THE PONIES ON THE SETTED DESCENT FROM INCHFIELD TO GAUXHOLME BEFORE CLIMBING WATTY LANE

and an escarpment, a sheer drop, even a precipice, on the other. Again, the wind has swept the edge clear of debris and, being a rock formation, the surface is hard. Consequently some packhorse tracks run along an edge and this location is known as a 'brink'. There are a number of brinks marked on the Ordnance Survey maps, and of course, we have the Top Brink pub overlooking Lumbutts. Stoodley Long Causeway coming from Halifax and Sowerby ran past the Top Brink, then turned left down a setted snicket to Lumbutts bridge. A very early track that pre-dated Woodhouse Road continued past Top Brink Farm and kept to on the north side of the stream in Causeway Wood, coming out at Woodhouse Mill. The road to Hebble End, Hebden Bridge and Haworth ran from the Top Brink up Lumbutts Lane, which has a guide stoop at the bottom.

THE STEEP CLIMB OF WATTY LANE FROM GAUXHOLME TO STONES

A perfect example of an edgeway is the Reddyshore Scout Gate running perilously close to a precipitous fall into the Walsden valley. On this brink we have the famous Allescholes milestone, from which the track to Halifax plunges down on a long rake to cross over the watershed at Bottomley just north of Warland.

Just to the north another edgeway known as Watty Lane climbs from the bottom of Pexwood Road at Gauxholme up to Watty Farm and Stones on its way to join Tower Causeway, the old road from Todmorden to Burnley.

Chapter 6 Peatlands

Peat is the *bête noire* of packhorse lore. Peat is like a living organism and, as such, in the past two hundred years has obliterated all evidence of packhorse tracks that were once on the surface. Not only do solid objects sink into its depths, but the creeping mass, which grows at the rate of some 1½ inches per century, envelops everything on its surface and then hides it beneath a canopy of cotton grass, molinia, heather or tufted clumps of mat grass. Consequently, out tracing a route, when one arrives at peat all is lost. Whole causeways have been swallowed up, leaving no sign of a beaten track, only a wild expanse of wasteland.

I learned two lessons about peatlands from unforgettable experiences. My companions and I were walking the old track from Dent along the eastern slopes of Crag Gill opposite Whernside until, after some few miles, I mused to myself that not only would this old hardcore road be easy meat for four-wheel-drive vehicles, it could easily have been negotiated by an ordinary family saloon, the surface being so good. Yet we only met walkers and the occasional cyclist. Then, without warning, we arrived at a covering of peat and the road could not have disappeared more abruptly had it fallen over a cliff. We were presented with a wilderness of peat bog, difficult to cross even on foot. On the Ordnance

MIKE RUSSELL EXCAVATING THE CAUSEWAY ON ROUGH HILL BETWEEN WATERGROVE AND INCHFIELD

39

Survey map the line of the road from here is only sketched in in dotted lines and the area is aptly named Foul Moss.

'Moss' is a word to add to the packhorse vocabulary, for it signifies a treacherous expanse of wet peat. Today, mosses have obliterated all signs of the routes used consistently over two hundred years ago. The packmen of those days must have dreaded the necessity of traversing these peatlands, and I am not sure quite how they achieved it. I can only presume that someone – the monks, the landowners or the parish – had laid and maintained a causeway or a temporary surface of catt. They found their way by waymarker cairns of small stones built into pyramids about a yard high. We had to cross Foul Moss by sinking almost to our knees in ooze. So much for the chances of a family saloon or even a four-wheel drive. Yet the packhorse achieved it, but the lesson is that trying to trace their routes over peatland is now impossible. I remember my despair in trying to determine the route from Reaps Cross via Raistrick Greave over to Widdop and being completely frustrated by an absolute loss of evidence under the Gorple peat.

When the upper reaches of the Gorple valley were inundated by Halifax Corporation in 1934, the water must have washed the peat away from the causeway from Raistrick Greave. In the drought of 1976 the water emptied to such an extent that the causeway stones were revealed like a skeleton lying on the floor of the reservoir to confirm the line of the route to Worsthorne.

Before the lower Gorple reservoir was built there was a large barn and farmstead at Reaps, the main business

REVEALED ON THE BOTTOM OF UPPER GORPLE RESERVOIR IN THE DROUGHT OF 1976, THE LOST CAUSEWAY ON THE ROUTE FROM WIDDOP TO WORSTHORNE

of which was to mow and reap the moorland grass between Reaps Farm and Reaps Cross. The resulting inferior crop was taken by the wagonload to be sold as fodder and bedding to hay and straw merchants in the industrial towns of East Lancashire and the West Riding. I can remember this poor-quality feed being sold in Burnley in the 1920s, although the trade died out soon after. But in the early years of the century Reaps and Reaps Cross were well-known locations for this somewhat dubious trade, of which both pack and draft horses were the victims.

Traversing peatlands taxed the ingenuity of early engineers. In 1830 George Stephenson had, in desperation, to float the world's first public railway, from Manchester to Liverpool, over Chat Moss on a raft of faggots. However, he was really using the methods of early turnpike road builders, such as John Metcalf, who floated the first Wakefield-Manchester turnpike road over Standedge on bundles of heather:

> One of the places was Pule and Standish common, being a deep bog, which he cast fourteen yards wide, and raised in a circular form. . . . Numbers of clothiers usually going that way to Huddersfield market, were not sparing in their censure, and held much diversity of opinion relative to its completion; but Metcalf got the piece levelled to the end, having sixty men employed there, he ordered them to pull and bind heather, or ling, in round bundles, and to lay it on the intended road in rows, and laying another across, pressing them well down; he then brought broad wheeled carriages (carts or waggons) to lead stone and gravel for covering. When the first load was laid on, and the horses had gone off in safety, the company huzzaed from surprise; they completed the whole of this length, which was about half a mile; and it was so particularly fine that any person might have gone over it in winter unshod, without being wet. This piece of road needed no repairs for twelve years afterwards.

(above and top right) THE CAUSEWAY ON INCHFIELD PASTURE PROVIDES A FIRM PASSAGE OVER PEAT MOOR

There are many hazards to travellers over peat moors. The inevitable run-off of rainwater erodes deep gullies down to the underlying clay. These gullies are far from uniform, both in direction and in depth, and at times form tunnels beneath the peat, while their top edges always have an overhanging fringe well covered with vegetation. They would have been an impassable barrier to the packhorse trains.

Large areas of peatland that are not free-draining become danger-

RAMSDEN LONG CAUSEWAY, CLEARED IN 1997

ous bogs in which animals and humans can be completely lost. Some bogs may be detected by an overgrowth of bog asphodel or of sphagnum moss. Others offer a quaking surface of temporary support but with hidden dangers beneath. Dry peat burns with intense heat and fires started in a drought sometimes smoulder at great depths for many months,

creating a pitfall for the unwary. I have heard of an incident in which a farmer and his horse and cart broke through and disappeared into one of these cavities.

I learned my second lesson about peatlands in a most unlikely place, on the very highest point of Pendle Hill. I had explored the massive bulk of the hill by walking along its top from the Nick to the Big End. I discovered that the plateau on the Big End was largely covered with wet peat which drained down into the Ogden Clough Water. This curves round gouging out a defile into the heart of the hill. With great difficulty I slipped and waded my way over the quagmire up to the popular tourist strip along the brink edge overlooking Barley. I was puzzled to find that this strip, for a distance of almost 100 yards back from the brink, was completely devoid of peat, was dry, hard and firm, and covered with a layer of stones of all sizes, some of which had been piled up by walkers into cairns or circular windbreaks. In past years I had noticed that even on calm days there was a considerable draught blowing over the edge. I now realized that this and the gales that frequently blasted the hill had dried out the peat and scoured it away down to the clay, leaving all the occluded stones deposited in place. In other words, dried peat will blow away after the manner of unwelcome blows over dried ploughland, or the disastrous dust storms of the American prairies. Winds that can sculpture huge blocks of millstone grit into fantastic shapes and scour out deep basins in their horizontal surfaces can easily achieve this effect of blow-away peat.

This revelation solved a mystery that had worried me when tracing the Limersgate over Cock Hill into

Luddenden Dean. Leaving that most delightful bridge at Lumb Falls, I had climbed up to the motor road from Hebden Bridge and located the gate through which the Ordnance Survey map marked the line of the Limersgate. A distinct path led off across a peat moor, but search as I might I could not find any trace of the usual attributes of a well-used packhorse track. There was no causeway or sign of there ever having been one, no holloway and no waymarkers. On either side was the usual wilderness of serrated peatland with all its hazards and peculiarities. Then, all at once, I realized that we were walking on a hard stony surface similar to the one on the top of Pendle Hill. Due to some freak of topography, the prevailing wind on this moor had created a swathe swept clear of peat. The ancient carriers had discovered this ribbon of good firm ground and incorporated it into their route from Lothersdale and the Boulsworth limestone hushings to the West Riding via Luddenden Dean. I stress that this was a freak occurrence, for the route was not a ridgeway, yet of course the same reasoning would apply to ridgeways.

This capability of peat to dry out and then blow away solved, for me, one other puzzle. When the Norman overlords partitioned vast areas of England into estates, they often delineated these by setting the serfs to work digging boundary mounds and ditches. These not only marked the boundary, but were made at such dimensions as to constitute 'deer leaps' to confine their herds. So very deep ditches were dug in order to throw up high mounds. But when one walks along the shallow remains of these once great ditches, there is never any trace of their associated mound. The answer is that these mounds, usually being on high ridges, had dried out and blown away.

Peatlands carry a variety of herbage of true grasses, sedges, rushes, heather and bog plants such as asphodel, myrtle and sphagnum. These pattern the peat moor with distinctive colours. Large areas are covered by the hare's tail and common cotton grasses, which in July and August are a riot of white heads, almost like snowdrops, presenting a dazzling white sheen which I call 'snow in summer'. My father told me that attempts had been made to spin this very fine silken cotton, but that these had all failed because the staple was too short. Areas of cotton grass can be traversed by laying a raised causeway.

However, this technique will not work with the expanses of tufted purple molinia that are also found on peat. These tufts, named 'clunters', grow so large – up to 3 feet in height – and are so dense that they are extremely difficult to negotiate, even on foot, and have defeated many attempts to cross them. The only way to make a track across clunters is to excavate down to firm ground. This was how Duke's Cut at Blackshaw Head was made, and the area of ground over which it runs is named Clunters on early maps. There are other 'cuts' in the same locality, including Eastwood Road, which is called The Cut in the Stansfield Township Highway Records. Both Duke's Cut and Eastwood Road were set out in the Stansfield Inclosure Award of 1816, but Duke's Cut – which was called Pole Hill and Slade Road in the award – is probably a much older track.

Rushes are another common feature of peatland, and in years gone by were extensively mown with the scythe for use as a floor-covering in castles, houses, palaces and churches. Certain varieties were much

All the above jobs were handwork, often done by the womenfolk, but today if work cannot be performed by a machine it is not done at all. Yet in the old days humans and packhorses could penetrate to areas where the modern tractor cannot go.

Peatland is of little agricultural use, and is the most difficult ground to reclaim or improve. Nevertheless, the pioneers of the inclosure years and the agricultural revolution walled them round and endeavoured to dry them out by digging regimented lines of deep trenches or 'grips'. But acidic peat defies all attempts to establish viable, productive, agricultural land, either for ploughing or grazing.

In my own parish of Cliviger there is an area of deep peat called Red Moss, which the Towneleys endeavoured to improve by walling round and gripping with trenches 6 feet deep. These trenches are remarkable for two reasons. One was that in an attempt to dry out the peat between the grips wooden drainage pipes were laid at a depth of about 3 feet. These were made of four wooden planks nailed together to form a 6-inch square section drainpipe which was drilled with 1-inch holes to admit water. Due to the preservative quality of peat, these are still to be found in good condition, and are a forerunner of earthenware pipes. The other fascinating feature of the Red Moss trenches is the many metal arrows that have been found, relics of the de Lacys' deer-hunting days.

Despite the difficulties it presents, peatland has provided a valuable asset for mankind in the form of the right of turbary enjoyed by the freeholders of the parish. This is the commoners' right to dig and carry away turves from the wastelands to use as fuel for cooking, heating water and keeping the house warm

THE ROUGH HILL CAUSEWAY BEFORE IT WAS OBLITERATED BY PEAT

sought by rich and poor alike for rushlights, which were the most common form of lighting. These were made by soaking rush pith in melted fat. There is a Rush Candle Clough on the West Riding side of Black Hameldon. Rushes were also dried and woven for a variety of uses.

Areas of peat moor where bracken has established itself are a brilliant green in early summer. In autumn, when the bracken has wilted to a delightful russet brown, it used to be scythed and carted to barns or made into stooks, for bedding young cattle in the winter time.

during the winter months. In summer there were extensive communal diggings out of which the peat was carved in rectangular blocks using specially shaped spades. The blocks were carefully stacked up with spaces between them to allow air to circulate, and left over the summer months to dry out, then carted, mostly by packponies, to the peat house. This was built against an outside wall of the farmhouse and had an opening leading directly into the kitchen where the all-important peat fire burned continuously.

I can recall, in my teens, taking the packhorse track over the bridge near the Brontë Falls, up past Lower and Middle Withens, which were then occupied, each with its peat fire burning, and up to Top Withens, which had only just been abandoned. This hilltop farmstead is thought to be the site of Emily Brontë's Wuthering Heights. My visit was in 1925, and Top Withens was then complete with all its rooms, roof and outbuildings intact. As a young boy I was most intrigued by the peat house against the back wall, with its yard-square hole through into the kitchen.

Dried peat was also used as animal bedding or litter in poultry houses, and as packing material for pottery. However, the deep black peat of the Pennines is far too acid for garden use, unlike the peat of the Somerset Levels, which is extensively mined, using narrow-gauge railtracks, for shipment all over the United Kingdom. But in former days individual house owners in the North had their own packpony or donkey for carting this most valuable necessity of life, and many limers' gals took return loads of peat into Lancashire, until transport by canals and railways made coal universally available. Nevertheless I can remember peat being hawked from door to door during the First World War when coal was rationed.

Peat is formed by the annual accretion of decomposed vegetation, which rots down each year to form a very fine layer. This process has gone on for thousands of years. The extreme antiquity of our peatlands is revealed on Blackstone Edge, where in the course of building the reservoir in the early nineteenth century the peat was found to be 25 feet deep.

I have described above some of the hazards that the packhorse teamsters had to circumvent over the extensive peatlands in the Pennines and elsewhere. Over the years safe routes were pioneered, but unfortunately all trace of them has been hidden by the moving peat and, in so doing, now presents an almost impossible task for the researcher.

Chapter 7 Waymarks, Signposts & Cairns

The practice of waymarking arterial routes of seasonal migration or incipient commerce goes back to Neolithic times six thousand years ago. The earliest routes were originally footways with men scouting ahead and the women acting as beasts of burden. It is possible that the clam bridge in Wycoller Dean and the remarkable cantilever bridge in Newsholme Dean were built to facilitate migratory passages through the Pennine chain via the Aire Gap. If so, these bridges indicate an advanced social order able to organize the construction of artefacts as impressive in their day as the canals and railways of the Industrial Revolution. The waymarkers of these prehistoric highways were sighting tumps, man-made notches on the skyline and incredible standing stones. However, the latter appear to have been more objects of a ritual pagan religion, more the goal at the end of a journey, than mere sighting stoops in themselves.

These ritual standing stones, named menhirs, are sometimes of an incredible size, such as the Devil's Arrows at Boroughbridge, and, as with the early bridges, one wonders how a Neolithic civilization transported and erected such wonders. In the South Pennines there is a remarkable example hiding in the corner of a field at Stones above Todmorden.

When, in much later times, our island became criss-

THE REMAINS OF COOMBE HILL CROSS AT THE HIGHEST POINT ON THE JUNCTION OF TRACKS FROM COLNE, COWLING AND HAWORTH

crossed with packhorse tracks, standing stones became the acknowledged waymarkers serving as sighting posts where a route ran over dreary, featureless terrain. These posts were erected along the line of the track on the brow of a hill so that they could be seen and followed from either direction. It is almost certain that the lay brothers of the monasteries quarried, transported and erected these stones at their chosen strategic positions.

It is not surprising then to find many of these sighting posts referred to as crosses and also to find

(left) WINDGATE NICK, LOOKING NORTH ACROSS WHARFEDALE, A NATURAL WAYMARK FOR DROVERS ON THEIR JOURNEY SOUTH FROM SCOTLAND

(below) ACCORDING TO JEFFERYS'S MAP OF YORKSHIRE (1775) THE ROAD THROUGH GILL GRANGE TO WEST MORTON WENT THROUGH THE NICK

true waymarkers and which were used for religious ceremonies. And, to compound matters, some have been adapted for both purposes, and even as market crosses for the sale of local produce. A typical example is Mount Cross above

that, if not actually sculptured into the form of a cross, they had crosses and in some cases religious inscriptions chiselled into their sides. A classic example of this is perpetuated on early Ordnance Survey maps showing the Long Causeway from Mereclough to Stiperden, where we had Stump Cross, Robin Cross, Maiden Cross, Duke's Cross and Stiperden Cross, of which only Stump and Maiden have escaped the vandalism of roadmakers and wall-builders. Also along this line, Towneley estate papers record a Standing Stone Height at the highest point near Causeway House. It is generally agreed that the monks of Whalley Abbey erected these so-called crosses as guides for packhorse trains carrying their wool crop to the east coast for shipment to Flanders.

However, as with all aspects relating to our subject, the student has to decide which standing stones are

Shore-in-Stansfield. This is a finely wrought Celtic cross of the type often ascribed to Paulinus. It could have been a boundary cross marking the boundary between the religious dioceses of York and Lichfield. However, in more modern times Mount Cross has been included in the Long Causeway series as a guidepost across the Stiperden valley. This has led to the belief that at some time it has been moved from its original position alongside the present road. However, it is equally legitimate to argue that perhaps the line of the road has moved, for Mount Cross stands alongside a possibly earlier route than the Long Causeway, for it is called Old Great Lane on a map in Calderdale Archives.

Many crosses were thrown down or even destroyed by the Puritans after the Civil War and some were removed and hidden by local families. As many as possible were replaced after the Restoration, but not necessarily in their original positions.

These are the problems facing the would-be researcher and can only be determined by a massive

REAPS CROSS ON HEPTONSTALL MOOR IN 1900. IT STANDS AT THE JUNCTION OF ROADS FROM COLNE, HEBDEN BRIDGE AND HAWORTH input of technology beyond the archaeological importance of the subject. It is for every standing stone to be classified according to the evidence presented by its associations with other indicators, such as the causeways and holloways of a known packhorse track.

With the increasing importance of packhorse transport to the national wellbeing from Tudor times onwards, Parliament became involved in assuring a progressive standardization and improvement in the networks throughout the kingdom. An Act of 1702 states one aspect very clearly:

STANDING STONE ON WHITE SLACK GATE

In parts of the Kingdom remote from towns there shall be, in every parish or place where two or more highways meet, erected a stone or post with an inscription of the nearest market town.

Having, by several Acts in the seventeenth century, made it the duty of local people to care for the highways in their parish, in the eighteenth century Parliament enacted a series of Acts for the compulsory erection of waymarkers, and then for upgrading these to signposts not only pointing out the way but naming the destination and the distances involved.

However, it was left to every parish highway surveyor to interpret the Acts and implement them according to the means at his disposal. So we have a refreshing variety of interpretations from parish to

parish. For example, the materials were not specified, so that stone, wooden and even iron signposts were erected. In upland areas such as the South Pennines stone was the most readily available material, so we have many survivals of the original posts erected in compliance with the Acts of Parliament. Wood, even oak, is of limited life and nearly all wooden posts have gone, whilst iron was of commercial value and could be melted down and used again, particularly in wartime. Fortunately the inscriptions on stonework have endured, a few now illegible but the majority well preserved. An interesting aside is that some confused surveyors interpreted one Act as meaning that the distances to the 'Capital City' had to be given, and so in a few rare examples we have the distance

THE SERIES OF GUIDEPOSTS ON THE PACKHORSE ROAD FROM ROCHDALE TO HALIFAX

THE ALLESCHOLES GUIDESTOOP SHOWS ROCHDALE 5 MILES, BURNLEY 9 MILES AND HALIFAX 10 MILES. THE DIRECTION TO TODMORDEN WAS ADDED LATER. THE STONE HAS BEEN BROKEN SEVERAL TIMES

THE SHURCRACK GUIDE STONE, HEYHEAD, NEAR LUMBUTTS, SHOWS ROCHDALE 6 MILES, BURNLEY 7 AND HALIFAX 9

THE TOP BRINK GUIDESTOOP RECORDS HALIFAX 8 MILES ON THE SOUTH FACE, AND HEPTONSTALL ON THE NORTH FACE. THE DISTANCE TO HEPTONSTALL IS UNDECIPHERABLE

given to London from a remote country location. For example, there is a signpost at Heptonstall Slack which reads: 'LONDON 220 MILES', a daunting journey for a packhorse team.

It was a customary rule in some areas that where a waymarker was inscribed with the name of a destination the direction of that destination was to the right of a traveller when facing the inscription. However, in other areas the inscription actually faced the destination, so a further Act of 1733 required that

the posts at cross roads should be true signposts actually pointing in the direction in which the traveller must go. It was no easy matter to comply with this directive when the waymarker was a solid block of millstone grit. The solution came very neatly by inscribing a hand with a finger pointing in the required direction. Thus was born not only the first generation of our modern signposts but an enduring collection of what became known as 'finger posts'. There are many fine examples of these in the West

Riding still serving this useful purpose, perhaps the best specimen being at Chapel House on the steep ascent from Hebden Bridge to Heptonstall. Also, I am happy to write, there are many survivors on the packhorse tracks of the pre-signpost era giving only the name and distance of a market town with no indication of which way to take, as we find on the famous Allescholes milestone.

We are fortunate that the West Riding county authorities based at Wakefield decreed from a very early date that all waymarkers should be substantial stone stoops. As a result, parishes vied with one another in not merely putting up rough stone slabs but in erecting finely dressed, four-sided, truncated pillars. In order to achieve their purpose as sighting posts, some of these were of such a height as to be of truly massive proportions, considering the portion buried in the ground. There is today the Long Stoop on the crest of Langfield Common, to be sighted both from Mankinholes and Lumbutts and from Withens Gate, and, possibly the finest, a splendid vertical post some 8 feet high above the long straight track of White Slack overlooking Lower Allescholes. Another fine example still stands alongside the Four Gates End on Duke's Cut at the junction with Moorcock Lane and its continuation into Noahdale. These are pure waymarkers with no

inscription and yet in themselves are wonderful examples of the stonemason's art.

On some routes a row of stone posts known as 'guides' was provided, possibly to delineate the track when hidden beneath a fall of snow. There are 'guides' marked on a sketch map of Gambleside in Rawenstall Library. And when John Fielden of Dobroyd built a carriage road over Langfield Edge he set up a set of four guides on the approach to Withens Gate, each carved as a miniature obelisk similar to the stone monument on Stoodley Pike.

In addition to man-made waymarkers, the teamsters used natural features in a continuation of the customs

THE DRAUGHTON FINGER POST AT THE CROSSROADS BETWEEN SKIPTON, ADDINGHAM, DRAUGHTON AND SILSDEN

HAWTHORNS ON THE TRACK THAT WINDS ROUND THE TOP OF RAWTONSTALL CLOUGH ABOVE MYTHOLM

promontories, were also used.

Over flatlands church towers and windmills served as sighting points. Also, lost in mysticism of a pagan era, there was a practice of planting three Scots firs in an elevated position on the line of a track, possibly to indicate a stopping place for drovers. In more modern times, a lone oak, elm, horse chestnut or beech was pressed into service to delineate the exact line. Even in the 1920s I remember my father leading a walk from Thornton-in-Craven to Malham on which a line of upstanding trees was used to find our way over extensive sheep pastures. I write this to emphasize how old customs persist into modern times.

On a much smaller scale, hawthorns and hollies were of the ancient wayfarers. Isolated hills and mountains on the skyline, such as Pendle Hill, were rough and ready guides from all points of the compass, and some of the highest locations, particularly those on which beacons had been maintained for times of national emergency (often named 'pikes'), became sighting points or even the meeting places of several routes. For more exact waymarkers, prominent knolls, nearly all marked on the Ordnance Survey maps and sometimes spelt 'knowls', became folklore and were used freely by locals instructing travellers on the best route to take. Knotts and scouts, being high overhanging sometimes planted in lines for the threefold duties of waymarkers, hedges and windbreaks. Very old and gnarled trunks still bearing red berries and a riot of white blossom in May will be found today alongside the packhorse tracks. I recall two examples on long-forgotten ways that impressed me greatly. One is on the little-known track from Todmorden to Sourhall, where a line of very ancient hawthorns must have not only provided welcome shelter for the teams as they emerged onto the high plateau but also pointed in a straight line the way to Todmorden Edge, Sourhall, and thence to the Tower Causeway on the pre-turnpike route to Burnley. The second example is a fine hedgerow of very old hawthorns sheltering the passenger on an elevated track between Winters Mill and Lower Rawtonstall above Mytholm.

Again I must stress that it is the gnarled appearance of these old hedgerows which must be looked for, indicating early boundaries or old rights of way. The forgotten name of these hedgerows was 'haigh' and an area inclosed from the wilderness by hawthorns rather than walls became known as the Haigh, Hague or Hagge, or possibly just Hag. This explains some of the placenames found on Ordnance Survey maps. However, 'hag' or 'hagg' can have other meanings, such as 'a wood', or even 'a rough, broken or boggy area', so it is necessary to interpret the meaning from the evidence on the ground.

Another form of waymarker was the cairn, built up in the shape of a pyramid by rough and ready drystone walling. I have recently seen written evidence confirming my belief that great slabs of stone were moved from the quarries to their destination on wooden rollers, being pulled by teams of horses. However, such a movement would require a good hard surface and where this was not present, such as over soft peat, it would not be possible to locate stone posts. Hence the use of cairns built from many small stones which could be gathered locally, or possibly transported to their location by the packhorse which they were intended to serve. So we find the cairn, or possibly just a pile of stones, marking the way over peatlands. In my boyhood, when wondering how to find our route from High Withens to Walshaw Dean, my uncle suddenly remembered that this track across the peat was marked by pyramid-like cairns, and so we discovered it to be.

Chapter 8 Gateposts, Ginnels & Turnbyes

A very surprising realization for me was that the now universally adopted five-barred gate swinging on strong hinge plates and gudgeons is a comparatively modern innovation. Apparently in early times the stonemasons and blacksmiths had not evolved a technique for securing an iron gudgeon pin to a stone gatepost. Indeed, the difficulty was so great that when the first toll roads were proposed, Parliament could not accept that adequate gates could be provided. At that time the 18-foot pike was the most fearsome weapon to repel cavalry, so the proposer said that he would mount pikes on swivels in such a way as to bring any rider or horsedrawn conveyance to a halt. Hence the generally adopted name of 'turnpikes' for the new toll roads. However, road builders soon came up with massive gateposts supporting gudgeons on which could be hung gates formidable enough to halt all except the most reckless daredevil such as Dick Turpin. But that these gates were something quite exceptional and very rare may be gauged from the fact that they gave a name to their locality, Lydgate, variations of which can be found in many parishes, based on the Norse *hlid*, meaning 'swing'.

With the success of the tollgates, blacksmiths came up with the idea of fixing gudgeons to stone posts by inserting the iron shank of the gudgeon into a hole in

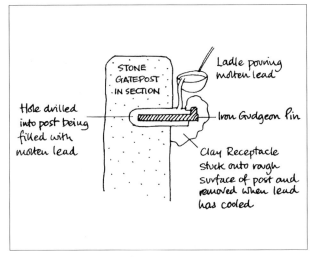

METHOD OF LEADING AN IRON GUDGEON PIN INTO A STONE POST

the stone post and pouring molten lead into the cavity. This was achieved by sticking a fireclay cup to the stone in such a way that the molten lead could be poured from a ladle into the cup, from which it ran into the hole and, on cooling, firmly soldered the iron to the stone. When cool, the clay was removed and the surplus lead chiselled away.

However, this was a post-turnpike technology. Before that more primitive gateways were contrived. The usual method was to chisel L-shaped grooves in

the opposing faces of a pair of stone posts and to cut wooden bars of exactly the correct length so that they could be inserted into the horizontal groove to fall down the vertical portion and thus be held in position. The drawback to this arrangement was that with, say, four bars to be laboriously removed and then replaced, the opening and closing of a gate was a lengthy business.

These crossbars were named 'stangs'. Every one had to be cut to an exact length to fit not only one particular gatehole but also its position in the gate between the two rough stone posts, which might vary in outline or which might not be truly parallel. Inevitably stangs would be broken and this presented a real problem of administration for the surveyor of highways. These gateways also presented a problem for the teamster, not only for the

(above and right) GATESTOOPS WITH GROOVES FOR STANG POLES. THE ONE ON THE RIGHT IS FROM NORMANDY, FRANCE

(below right) IN THIS EXAMPLE FROM CUMBRIA THE STANGS ARE SLOTTED THROUGH HOLES IN THE GATESTOOP

tedious hold-up but, when harried by a herd of curious

cattle, he had to get his train through without the cattle following and so straying from their summer pasture. This could cause friction with the freeholders who had grazing rights over the wastes. It is recorded that the packmen carried cudgels to defend themselves in case of trouble.

This problem of curious cattle and the difficult gateway also meant that a teamster had to have two or three helpers, usually teenage boys and sometimes girls, and also a good dog to keep the cattle at bay. Lone wayfarers often joined up with packhorse trains for mutual protection as

footpads and even small gangs of outlaw robbers would beat up and rob defenceless travellers in lonely places. These wayfarers were only too happy to assist the teamster in any way they could and particularly in opening and closing these awkward gateways. It is obvious that two men could remove and replace these heavy poles far more quickly than a youth struggling on his own.

A variation upon the L-shaped slot was to drill a line of holes in the posts and slide the stangs through them. These were not as secure as the slots and the poles could be brought down by animals rubbing against them.

Although no longer in use, there are hundreds of these stang-pole gateposts still standing in the countryside – I even have a pair on my farm in Cliviger – for their use was not restricted to the packhorse tracks. Nevertheless, the best examples are still seen on these tracks and help greatly in tracing routes where all trace of the track itself has been

obliterated by vegetation.

Most gateways are some 10 feet wide, but I have been puzzled to find some as narrow as 2 feet, through which a pack animal could not pass. These narrow gateways are usually in the side walls separating the track from farmers' fields, and one explanation which I can offer is that they were used for the recovery of strays which were wandering on the packhorse track. I don't think they were for humans because any number of stockproof stiles were available for them.

Although most gateposts are massive slabs of sandstone or millstone grit, in some localities tall wafers of slate are used, the best of course being those of the true blue slate. These are positioned with their wide flat surfaces facing each other to form a gateway

(above) GATESTOOP WITH SQUARE HOLE ON THE TRACK AT GRAINING WATER, WIDDOP, AND *(below)* ON BEAUMONT CLOUGH ROAD NEAR HORSEHOLD

some 2 feet in depth, and they are thin enough to be drilled right through with all the necessary fittings bolted in place with nuts and washers. There are many examples of these on the plateau of Hapton High Park.

The next puzzle is the large number of massive millstone gateposts with a large square hole cut right through. Whereas the stang slots are chiselled into that face of the posts which is along the line of the route, these square holes are usually cut through the face that is at right angles to the direction of travel. They are about 6-8 inches square and some 5 feet

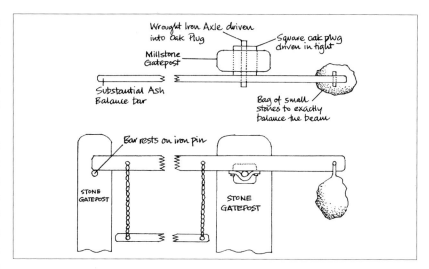

METHOD OF FITTING A BALANCE BEAM TO A STONE GATESTOOP – A POSSIBLE EXPLANATION FOR THE STOOPS WITH SQUARE HOLES THAT ARE STILL FOUND TODAY

above the original trackbed. Their purpose has yet to be proved by concrete evidence, for no one living today has the necessary memories or recollections of other than the square hole in a stone post. Nor has any painting, woodcut or lithograph yet turned up illustrating one of these posts in use.

I have been told that these holes were for mounting strong wooden blocks which themselves served as mountings for iron axles for carrying a balance beam that could be raised and lowered quickly across the track. We have already seen the difficulty that the early artisans had in securing iron gudgeon pins to the stone posts. Imagine the problem presented by supporting a heavy balance beam in such a manner as to give reliable service and withstand the rigours of our climate over many years. The problem could have

been given to the cartwrights, who knew all about contriving axles and wheels for the ox wains of the day. A wooden block with an iron stub-axle, exactly the same as one half of the axle beam of a wagon, with a balance beam rotating on it with the same bearing as the wagon wheel would offer a foolproof and reliable solution. These balance beams would have been exactly the same in function as the modern ones at railway level-crossings, and the speed with which they could be operated would have been a godsend to the harassed packhorse men. The wooden blocks had to be made out of a hardwood such as oak or elm which would not swell by absorbing moisture and so burst the gatepost.

Only local materials could be used in packhorse days, and I have heard of such beams balanced on the

GINNEL AT POT OVEN, CLIVIGER, BEFORE
RESTORATION

routes have become impassable swamps infested with rank grass and rushes, in which the walker can sink to knee level in waterlogged humus, the accumulation of two hundred years' neglect.

Somewhere beneath this mass will be found the original trackbed, possibly a fine run of causeway stones, and also a stone drainage system of considerable ingenuity. Unfortunately, such systems are prone to silting up unless regularly cleared out. Even drove roads over 40 feet wide are subject to this problem. An extreme example used to be found on the Moorbottom Road along the base of Boulsworth Hill in Trawden where today the route passes below Brink Ends Farm before dropping down and fording Turnhole Clough. This was obviously intended as a drove road to guide herds of Scotch cattle through the Wycoller Dean inclosures after their overnight stop in the Herders' Inn pastures, for it is some 44 feet wide and walled on either side for a quarter of a mile through otherwise dry pastures. However, the walls so dammed up the drainage that the whole length and width became an impassable swamp, yet at either end where it is not walled there was a good dry hardcore road surface.

Walled broadgates and narrowgates through parish farmlands have already been mentioned, but there is a variety of these that are named 'ginnels' or 'snickets'. These are found where a narrowgate negotiates a difficult patch of countryside and has required some primitive civil engineering to make a way. This could be a cutting through a headland, a tortuous track over broken land, or perhaps a climb between hillside pastures. An example of the first is my own Cliviger ginnel near Pot Oven Farm, which cuts through a

outboard end by a willow basket carrying just the required weight of small stones, a neat solution to a tricky problem.

Many routes are confined between stone walls for at least part of the way. Of necessity the foundations of these walls must go down to a firm base. Consequently they form linear dams that, unless drainage is provided, prevent the natural escape of rainwater and flood the trackway. Today many of these

knoll for some 70 yards, with 6-foot high retaining walls and cobbled bottom. All these ginnels are almost completely stone-girt, such as the best known, the Buttress, which leads from Heptonstall to the packhorse bridge in Hebden Bridge town centre. Its continuation is the Snicket, which leads up to the Wadsworth Road. A particularly fine example is the sunken ginnel climbing up the end of Whalley Nab on a track from Whalley to Great Harwood. This latter was probably built by the lay brothers of Whalley Abbey. A less meticulous example is the crazy enclosed causeway from Bottomley through to North Hollingworth Farm, just above Walsden, which is now part of the South Pennine Packhorse Trails Trust's 35-mile bridleway route from Marsden to Haworth. The walker will come across many of these tightly stone-girt passages which, as opposed to the straight and even narrowgates through cultivated fields, take the trunk routes through difficult and broken countryside.

Anticipating the railways by many years, there were even tunnels on the well-used tracks. When the Farrer family landscaped their Ingleborough estate, which was crossed by the packhorse route from what was, in sailing-ship days, Lancashire's most important sea port, Lancaster, over the Pennines into Richmondshire, they diverted the track through a series of stone-lined tunnels from the village of Clapham out onto the limestone moors. There is also a tunnel beneath the relatively modern road from Weasel Hall to Old Chamber to accommodate the early track that forded the Calder at Hebble End, Hebden Bridge, on its way via Cragg Vale to Saddleworth. This was used by packhorses carrying lime from Lothersdale.

Water, particularly running water, is the enemy of road surfaces. It softens the substrata, resulting in huge potholes and deep ruts on level going. In the hills rainwater gathers itself into gushing torrents, washes away the hardcore surfaces and gouges out deep gullies. The only road surfaces to stand up to rainwater are the enduring pavements of the packhorse causeways and those which have been

DRAINAGE SYSTEM ON THE MAGNA VIA, HALIFAX. THE DRAIN, COVERED BY STONE FLAGS, RUNS DOWN THE RIGHT-HAND SIDE OF THE ROAD TO A TURNBYE, WHICH CARRIES WATER ACROSS THE ROAD

STONECRACKER JOES (from George Walker, *The Costume of Yorkshire*, 1814)

as quickly as they could after every deluge, endeavouring to camber the surface so that the water would hopefully run off into the ditches on either side of the road. But much of the water preferred obstinately to stay on the road itself.

Those packhorse tracks that had been upgraded to hardcore cartways suffered the most. One remedy on hills was to provide a series of turnbyes or bywashes at an angle across the road to gather up the water and run it into a stone-flagged gutter down the roadside. These turnbyes were constructed of stone kerbs or small flags set on edge with a stone channel on the uphill side and were strategically placed wherever the camber of the roadway changed to deflect the water off to the side. This prevented a torrent of water building up and washing down the road itself, possibly ripping out the surface.

With the advent of wheeled transport turnbyes became most unpopular. They presented no problem to horses, but to the motorist they were obstructions that resulted in broken springs. There are thousands of turnbyes remaining on routes no longer used by wheeled transport other than the mountain bike. They are still the most effective way of turning water off a sloping track.

paved for their full width with stone setts. The hundred of miles of hardcore roads which were the precursors of the tarred macadam and Trinidad asphalt of the motor age had no defence against the onslaught of water. Every length was either maintained by local farmers or, for the more important roads, by stone-breakers. These men, known as Stonecracker Joes, were given piles of quarry stone and beautifully balanced hammers, with a specially shaped wrought-iron head held by a long cherrywood handle, which they could wield all day long without tiring. They spent their whole lives by the roadside cracking the stone into macadam-sized pieces. They were given the responsibility for a certain length of roadway and filled in the potholes and ruts

NORTHWELL LANE FROM HEPTONSTALL TO NEW BRIDGE, MIDGEHOLE, RETAINS FINE STRETCHES OF ORIGINAL PAVING *(left)* AND STONE TURNBYES *(right)*

Their construction depended upon the materials available and upon the ingenuity of the constructor. Consequently, like farmers' field gates, every one is different, and this endless variety can be a source of delight to the crackpot who is obsessed by such things.

The term 'bywash' was adopted by the canal engineers to denote a flagged overflow leading from a channel down into a river or stream to take flood water, performing exactly the same function as the turnbyes on packhorse tracks.

Chapter 9 Overnight Stopping Places

I have come across many little stone watering troughs on the packhorse ways, located where a never-failing spring conveniently provides a supply of glistening clear water. Just to watch this run in and then out again from a notch chiselled in the stone is a sheer delight. But, I have thought, however could a train of up to thirty ponies drink from such a small trough? My conclusion is that these were only provided for the passer-by whose riding horse was steamed up on oats, bran and hay, all dry fodder. The packhorse ponies were fed solely on grass; economics would not permit bought-in provender. With a belly full of grass the ponies did not require much

THE SET OF WATER TROUGHS IN MANKINHOLES, NEAR TODMORDEN. THE CIRCULAR TROUGHS AT EITHER END WERE USED FOR COOLING MILK CHURNS AS LATE AS THE 1970s

additional moisture, except perhaps on very hot days when they were allowed to snatch a drink when fording a stream. The long troughs that are often attributed to the packhorse trains were undoubtedly for dairy cattle. Before the advent of automatic watering bowls, in winter, the cows were loosened out of their shippens after milking time to drink at the spring-fed water trough. This could be a very time-consuming task for the farmer if only one or two cows at a time could drink from a small trough. Hence the provision of these long troughs. Invariably these are

THIRTEEN HUNDRED FEET ABOVE SEA LEVEL, THE STOODLEY PUBLIC SLAKE TROUGH

PACKPONY WITH BELLS AND MUZZLE, BEAMISH

Lincolnshire. However, the packhorses gleaned their sustenance from the wayside when resting (being muzzled for the journey) and fertilized it in their passing.

Although the ponies would snatch a bite at every opportunity, most of their grazing was during the night when they had been relieved of their burdens. Here again the teamster had to do some precise planning and timekeeping. Like today's long-distance lorry driver, once he left his home farm the teamster could be away on his travels for many days. The ideal situation was to arrive at his destination in the late afternoon, unload, off-saddle and turn the ponies loose onto whatever pasture was available. Then early the following morning the team would be saddled and hurry off to the next pick-up assignment. Because of these exacting time schedules the ponies were always driven at a fast pace.

When the train could not reach its destination before nightfall or before the ponies had been driven to the limit of their endurance, an overnight stopping place had to be reached where the panniers could be stored in a safe place, preferably under cover. There, in addition to the welfare of the horses, the people accompanying them had to be fed and rested. Consequently, farms that specialized in this service were well known to the packman as good overnight resting places with pastures set aside for grazing. The charge for the grazing was ½d per beast per night, so these pastures were named Halfpenny Pasture, and the lane leading to them Halfpenny Lane. There is such a lane named today across the Garstang Road from the

only found alongside a farmstead, and it is only a coincidence should they also be on a packhorse route.

Large water troughs were provided by the thousand outside the hostelries and in the market towns and centres of the Industrial Revolution. However, these were for the working horses, which were fed exclusively on dry rations. I can well remember in my boyhood the trusses of hay and nosebags of oats and bran carried by every cabby and carter in the early 1920s. In consequence the draught horses defecated every few hundred yards and armies of road sweepers were constantly at work. The sweepings were picked up by refuse carts and off-loaded into canal barges at special manure wharves, for delivery to the potato-growing fields near Ormskirk or even sent by rail to

Alston Arms in Longridge. The grazing fields were also called horse pastures, so that the whole set-up was called Horse Pasture Farm, like the derelict one today above Cranberry Dam on White Slack Gate.

Also in many parishes there are small farms named Windy Harbour to which the packhorse trains could go for shelter. There are two Windy Harbours quite near my home both available from the Long Causeway. As the name implies, these were sheltered locations and so were sometimes a little distance off the main track which would be exposed to all the wind and rain which our climate could subject them to. Our Cliviger Windy Harbour was some half a mile down into the valley in a location named Hellyplatt, which means 'a hidden place'. The other Windy Harbour is in Stansfield, just below Long Causeway above Whirlaw, but examples can be found all over the Pennines.

Another name for these overnight pastures was Bell Close, and the attendant buildings called Bell House on account of the constant tintinnabulation of the bells that swung from iron hoops on the packhorses' collars, both as a warning – anticipating the bicycle bell – and also to help locate the grazing animals in the early-morning mists. There is a Bell House today on the formerly busy track from Hebble End in Hebden Bridge over to Saddleworth. This Bell House is high above Cragg Vale on the edge of Bell House Moor.

The meaning of words changes with the centuries. In early times a 'hospital' or 'hospice' was a place of rest for weary travellers and attached to these was a pasture for the all-important beast of burden, the horse. Dialect has corrupted these to 'spitalfields' and this name was still in use when the hospitals had been transmuted into hostelries or wayside inns. There was such a spitalfield next to the Roebuck Inn in Portsmouth between Burnley and

WINDY HARBOUR AND WINDY HARBOUR LANE ON THE NORTH SIDE OF THE CALDER VALLEY. SITED BETWEEN LONG CAUSEWAY AND UPPER LANE, IT LIES ON A LOST ROUTE LEADING FROM ROCHDALE INTO YORKSHIRE

HORSEHOLD, ON THE VALLEY SHOULDER ABOVE HEBDEN BRIDGE – A STOPPING PLACE FOR THE PACKHORSE TRAINS

Todmorden, and, being on the pre-turnpike road which ran up past Bearnshaw Tower to Sourhall, no doubt it was grazed by the packponies.

Every civilization or tribe of mankind has, throughout the ages, had to find a source of salt or else perish. In the isolated communities of the Pennine chain a regular supply of salt was a vital necessity and, being so necessary not only to maintain life but to increase the enjoyment of food, it is not surprising to find that the salters were the most popular of packhorse men. They were welcomed everywhere and special provision was set aside for the overnight welfare of their teams. Names including the word 'salt' are far away the most prolific ones along the packhorse tracks. Indeed, by connecting up salt names on the Ordnance Survey maps W. B. Crump was able to trace the salt routes radiating out from Cheshire, as described in his paper 'Saltways from the Cheshire Wiches' for the Lancashire and Cheshire Antiquarian Society in 1939. I am not saying that he was able to do this without some investigations in the field, but such is the plenitude of salt names that it could just have been possible. On the subject of overnight stopping places, for the horses there were Saltersfields, Salter Ings, Salter Furlongs, Salter Flatts and Salter Closes, and for the men Salthouses, Salter Crofts and Salter Barns.

A place named Baitings was also a stopping place, especially for feeding, whether for human or horse or both is not quite clear. 'Bait' is a very common word among working-class people for the food taken to work in a 'bait box', often a prized item of leather with good fastenings to prevent the ingress of mice, rats, or even dogs. The word is also in common use today by fishermen. Part of the historic Blackstone Edge packhorse road on its descent to Ripponden is called Baitings Gate, and there is a Baitings Gate Pasture alongside the route.

Certain isolated farms on the packhorse tracks had bread ovens built into the very fabric of the house walls and I have been assured that these were in regular use to bake bread which the teamsters took with them on their travels. Such ovens are still *in situ* at Hartley Royd on Ridge Gate (now called Bluebell Lane), the track from Shore to Heptonstall, and at South Hollingworth just off the saltersway from Rochdale to Halifax.

When I first came to Middle Pasture Farm in 1947 the old inhabitants of the district referred quite often to a small drystone building in the corner of Roger Pasture, some 50 yards in from Maiden Cross, as the Saddling Cote. This was at the junction of east-west and north-south packhorse routes. Unfortunately the stone from this building was used as roadstone by contractors on the opencast coal workings in 1954. However, its name suggests to me that other barn-like buildings, such as the one on Boulsworth's Moorbottom Road named Beaver Cote, could have been a rendezvous for packhorse trains for easing the weight off the ponies' backs or even for exchanging loads in the way of business.

There was a similarity in lifestyles between the packhorse men and the cattle drovers, and they must have often intermingled in their daily journeys. One wonders whether the tradition that the drovers slept outdoors wrapped in a blanket or plaid was also true of the packhorse men, perhaps using the horse blankets and saddles as impromptu mattresses and pillows, to keep expenditure to an absolute minimum. It was the dealers and traders who rested in inns and slept in the feather beds. For the teamsters a saddling cote had to be sufficient.

Chapter 10 The Inclosure of the Commons

By Tudor times, in the sixteenth century, with the emergence of a dominant government, the countryside was ripe for development and the Agricultural Revolution not too far ahead. At this time the farmlands of each parish were held by the so-called freeholders in closely grouped nucleated villages. These freehold lands were surrounded by large areas of wasteland, also called commons or moors. The wastelands were necessary to the villagers for their economic and domestic survival so, although these wastes belonged to the Lord of the Manor, the freeholders were granted six rights of common on them: pasture, pannage, estovers, turbary, piscary and common in the soil. Pasture meant that each freeholder could have summer grazing for a number of animals proportional to his freehold acreage. Pannage was the right to allow pigs to root over certain areas, particularly woodland for beech mast, acorns and roots of weeds such as nettles. Estovers was the right to take dead wood or small branches, either for fuel or repairing fences and buildings, along with litter such as bracken or rushes for bedding. Turbary was the right to dig and take away turf, usually peat, for fuel. Piscary was the right to take fish, while common in the soil was the right to take sand, gravel, stone or minerals. All these rights were only for the use of the commoners themselves; they could only use the feed for their own animals, the fish for their own household, and wood and stone on their own holding.

With freedom from internal strife and increasing prosperity, the freeholders wanted to add to their farmed land, and initially they did this by encroachment upon the commons. They fenced in an area of adjacent waste and incorporated it into their cultivated acres. Becoming aware of this, the Lord of the Manor instituted surveys to ascertain the land use within his jurisdiction. Wherever an encroachment could be proved, the freeholder had to pay for it. The surveys instituted a new system known as compounding by which the freeholder and the Lord of the Manor compounded for the freeholder to take over and inclose a certain area of wasteland and to pay a rent for it, so acknowledging that his new land was not freehold. This arrangement suited both parties, for the farmer acquired more land to cultivate and the lord had an increased rent roll. Very shrewdly the Manor retained the mineral and sporting rights, and with the Industrial Revolution large fortunes were made from royalties on the extraction of coal, metallic ores and fireclay.

We are not concerned here with the inclosure of the townfields or village greens, only with inclosure of the wasteland, which so affected the packhorse routes.

After the initial tentative inclosure of small areas into

(above) EXTRACT FROM THE INCLOSURE AWARD FOR STANSFIELD (1816) SETTING OUT NOAH DALE ROAD. THE INCLOSURE PLAN (below) SHOWS THE AWARDED ROADS, ALLOTMENTS, NAMES OF ALLOTTEES AND ACREAGE OF EACH ALLOTMENT

the freehold holding, in the sixteenth century the Lord of the Manor started to offer considerable areas of moor for compounding with parish freeholders for them to inclose, improve and add to their existing holdings. The new land was not granted freehold but was retained under the control of the Manor Court under an arrangement that became known as copyhold. After the transaction had been completed, the allotment holder was given a copy of the details of his new holding as written down in the Court Rolls of the Manor. This 'copy' became his title deed to the land.

In the seventeenth and eighteenth centuries a procedure evolved in which a commissioner was appointed to administer the process of inclosure. Where there was complete agreement between tenants and lord, a private inclosure award, ratified by an entry in the Court Rolls of the Manor, was carried out at minimum expense. However, if difficulties were expected, the Lord of the Manor applied for an Act of Parliament. There was little difference between a private and a parliamentary award, except that the latter had a legal basis which could not be ignored and which is still in force today.

In both categories the commissioner's main task was to allot a specified area of the wastes to each freeholder in proportion to his freehold acreage. This division of the hitherto open moorland into inclosures interfered with the public's right to go over them in all

DUKE'S CUT, SET OUT IN THE STANSFIELD AWARD AS A PRIVATE CARRIAGE ROAD

directions. Consequently the commissioner had first to set out rights of way to run between the new inclosures. He then prepared a map of the details of the inclosure, showing where the new roads ran and new fields to be allotted. In the case of a private award, these were thrashed out and agreed at sessions of the courts of the Manor. In the parliamentary awards, once these were sanctified, the details on the map and in the award became the law of the land.

We are only concerned here with the rights of way. These were of two categories – public and private. The private roads were to give all the freeholders access to their new fields and had to be maintained out of a rate levied on the freeholders concerned in proportion to their acreage. The public roads took the ancient King's Highways, the packhorse tracks and the drove roads,

SHEDDEN DROVE ROAD, SET OUT IN THE CLIVIGER AWARD OF 1808 AS THE WORSTHORNE ROAD, A PUBLIC CARRIAGE ROAD 33 FEET WIDE

maintained out of the parish rate, through the new inclosures. The roads, both public and private, became known as 'inclosure roads' and had to be walled or fenced in the same manner as the new fields. The commissioner stated in the award the status of these roads, i.e. horseway, cartway, driftway, etc., and in all cases specified a minimum width, possibly less for a horseway, but upwards of 30 feet for a public

carriageway or driftway. This surprising width has proved fortuitous in modern times for it has been possible to upgrade these roads without having to rebuild the boundary walls.

As award followed award, their effect upon the packhorse routes was profound. Instead of branching out in all directions, the tracks were now confined into walled-in routes as far as the latest moor gate opening

(above and below right) LONDON ROAD ON LANGFIELD COMMON, A MOOR-FENCE TRACK DATING FROM THE NINETEENTH CENTURY

caused by cheap imports, the practice of inclosing and improving the moorlands ceased completely in the nineteenth century. The end of this phase of land management left the rural scene in a vastly different state from that of the early days of packhorse transport in the sixteenth and early seventeenth centuries. Then comparatively small areas of farmed and inclosed land were surrounded by vast tracts of open wastelands over which the packhorse tracks radiated in all directions. By roughly the middle of the nineteenth century the position was reversed, with nearly all land granted into private ownership and inclosed. This meant that the greater part of a journey was along inclosure roads, which varied in width and construction with each succeeding award, followed by a shorter journey over what remained of the wastelands. The new routes through the inclosures did not necessarily follow the old tracks, so upon arriving at the latest moor gate the teamster had to locate the old track over the wastes.

onto the wastes. The old routes were now lost in the farmers' fields. In the case of private awards, these were illegally closed by the landholder since only Parliament had the power to extinguish a right of way. So today we may find abandoned causeways over private land with no right of way given on the modern definitive maps or possibly only marked as footpaths when due to past use they should clearly be bridleways. In the case of the parliamentary awards, the commissioner had the power not only to create new rights of way but also to extinguish old ones. So it would appear that ancient tracks in these cases are lost for ever as rights of way unless some form of concessionary rights can be negotiated with the landowners.

Due to the catastrophic decline in British agriculture

This was achieved by skirting the new inclosure to find the old route. Consequently, in the declining years of packhorse transport 'moor-fence tracks' often produced holloways along the moorland side of the inclosure walls.

Moor-fence tracks, whether designated by that name or not, still remain today often as holloways particularly over peat moors. One such runs over Heptonstall Moor towards Raistrick Greave, and another, part of the Limersgate from Sharneyford to Wardle, on the western slope of Brown Wardle Hill. There are others too numerous to mention.

Another manner in which the old routes have been lost is the result of the many Acts of Parliament sanctioning the creation of water-storage reservoirs with their attached water-gathering ground. Where every endeavour is made to contrive alternative routes, these are not the original packhorse ways. This problem is particularly rife in the South Pennine hills where numerous reservoirs have been built to provide the water supplies to the industrial towns of Lancashire and the West Riding. These multiple areas of water catchment land fragment what would otherwise be carriers' trunk routes, such as were in constant use by the limers, and salters of the seventeenth and eighteenth centuries when this land was open moor with rights of way in all directions.

Today all but very small patches of these erstwhile commons are now in private ownership, with their owners well aware of the extinction of the packhorse tracks over their land either by the past two hundred years of dereliction or more absolutely by various Acts of Parliament.

Yet these long-disused routes are still there on the ground. Luckily many of them retain a public right of way, although far too many are only recorded as footpaths.

Chapter 11 Packhorse Vocabulary

Packhorse transport having persisted as a national institution for hundreds of years, it is inevitable that it developed its own vocabulary.

The *Oxford English Dictionary* derives the words of the modern English language from several root languages such as Latin, Old English, Anglo-Saxon, Norse and Norman French. Consequently, it is usual to find certain words peculiar to regions which were predominantly settled by certain national groups. In the Pennines we find the influence of Ancient British from Elmet, Wales and Strathclyde, Anglo-Saxon from the general infiltration of Angles and Saxons in the Dark Ages, Danish from the Danelaw or Midland kingdom of Mercia, and Norse from the Scandinavians who tamed the hills and valleys of the Pennines and the Lake District. As an example, Dr T. D. Whitaker in his *History of Whalley* gives a list of the different words used north and south of the River Ribble: to the south are found words of predominantly Danish or of Anglo-Saxon origin, while to the north are words of pure Scandinavian.

So, before the advent of a national education system and the BBC, there were distinct differences in pronunciation and vocabulary from one locality to another. In my own Lancashire there were distinct variations in speech between districts as near as Burnley, Blackburn and Rossendale. Before the peoples of England were mixed up by the industrial revolution, there were even easily recogized differences in the physical appearances of the settled population.

PACKPONIES CARRYING BOLTS OF CLOTH ON THE ASCENT TO THE NICK OF PENDLE

When, around the turn of the eighteenth century, the government embarked on a cartographic survey of the countryside to give our gunners an advantage over that master of the use of artillery, Napoleon, should his invasion succeed, they called it the Ordnance Survey. The surveyors did a most remarkable job, not only in mapping accurately all features such as rivers, valleys, hills, roads and towns, but also in recording in great detail the names in use at that time of every locality and physical feature. They did this by questioning the local people and giving a phonetic spelling of their own to the natives' pronunciation. This can easily be imagined for the environs of towns, villages and hamlets, but amazingly all areas of the wastelands are also named in great detail. The only people familiar with the unenclosed moors were the commoners, who had rights of grazing, turbary and estovers over the common wastes attached to their parish, and the packmen and women and drovers, who used the rights of way that crossed them. These travellers would need to name every feature so as to communicate with their colleagues in the normal everyday pursuit of their livelihood. The packmen and drovers could be of any ethnic background, even Gaelic-speaking Scots, giving strange names which nevertheless the local people took to and adopted. Consequently the words gathered by the Ordnance surveyors in each district were predominantly of that district's vernacular with a few 'foreign' ones mixed in. The itinerants therefore had a considerable influence in the formation of the English language by distributing their chosen descriptions throughout the realm.

This explains why certain names in a district were

SALTER RAKE GATE, A ROUTE ORIGINATING IN SAXON TIMES FOR THE CARRIAGE OF SALT FROM CHESHIRE

Amongst this welter of strange dialects and differing physical types, the packman moved as a stranger. He had a strange appearance and an even stranger dialect, but, with that facility of countryfolk to adapt and adopt so long as they wished to do so, there was no lack of understanding between them.

derived from more than one of the root tongues, and also why certain names were common to all districts, despite the different origins of the inhabitants.

Apart from the naming of natural features, the packmen and drovers developed words appertaining to their trade, and these words, being in use for hundreds of year, have passed into the English language, some in everyday use and others comparatively obscure.

Far and away the commonest word associated with the packhorse era is the word 'causeway'. This has survived into modern times, being used as a title for natural locations or specific buildings, but all having in commmon their relationship to an ancient causeway. Thus we have Causeway Head, Causeway End, Causeway Side, etc., as locations, and Causeway House, Causeway Cottage or Causeway Mill for buildings. And I have already mentioned the ubiquitous Long Causeway which is still used to name stretches of modern motor roads.

For today's reader, educated to a standard curriculum, the greatest confusion is caused by the word 'gate'. The modern interpretation is that this is a device for opening or closing an entrance. To the settlers of Scandinavian origin in the west of England the word 'gate', from the Old Norse *gata* meaning 'a way', meant 'a road'. To the English peoples the word, derived from Old English *geat*, meant a barrier which could be opened or closed, as in the modern meaning. So in the Pennines, roads or tracks were often named 'gates'. Even today in my own town of Burnley the main road from the west is called Westgate, and there used to be an Eastgate, now called Yorkshire Street.

Which brings us to the main Roman roads being named 'streets'. This name was not perpetuated by the Anglo-Saxons, who used the word 'way', so we have 'highways' and 'byways'; but for some reason individual ways leading out of towns or villages were most commonly called 'lanes', perpetuated today in our 'traffic lanes'. Another but much rarer name was 'alle', from the French *aller*, 'to go'. This was usually given to the common way out of the inclosures onto the commons, later 'alleyways'. So we have Allescholes, 'the settlement on the road'. However, this word, now spelled 'alley', changed its meaning to denote a quiet backwater in the poorer parts of a city, as exemplified in Gracie Fields's song from the film *Sally in Our Alley*. The word 'road' was little used before the turnpike era but was then adopted and became the general term into the motor age. However, our most modern trunk routes have reverted to the original Anglo-Saxon 'way' as 'motorways', so the general use of 'road', 'street', 'lane' and 'way' is all jumbled up today.

Tracks were associated with rough pathways through virtually unexplored countryside over which the hooves of the horses left a 'track'. This term would appear to be a comparatively modern appellation for a packhorse way, reflecting the modern image of these ways being over a wild and lonely wilderness. But I have no knowledge of this word being used when the wastelands were alive with packhorse gangs and drovers' herds. To modern ears 'track' has become more associated with railways all over the world.

A 'jag' was a load, and the man who moved the loads was named a 'jagger'. Depending on the physical condition of the ponies, the average load for all commodities was 2 cwt (224 lb), i.e. 1 cwt in each

JAGGER PONIES LEISURELY WEND THEIR WAY. THE LEAD HORSE WEARS AN ORNATE COLLAR AND BELLS

pannier, so it required a gang of ten ponies to transport 1 ton. A horse-load became accepted as a unit of weight on invoices and cost accounts for bulk materials such as lime, sand, coal and iron ore. It is probable that more valuable staples had to be check-weighed.

The packponies were of any of the sturdy forest, moor or hill breeds, such as the New Forest, the Dartmoor and the Welsh, but in the Pennines the preferred breed was the Galloway, so much so that packhorses were called 'gals' whatever their origin. This term was then applied to the roads used by packhorses, for example, Galloway Gate or Gallgate. I have even come across references to 'Galloway roads' in estate papers.

After almost two hundred years of disuse, many packhorse tracks still have their working-day names and are marked as such on the Ordnance Survey maps. This applies particularly to limers' and salters' ways. There are scores of Limersgates, Limers' Lanes, Salterfords, Salfords and Salter Rakes, well known to ramblers today.

The saltways originally ran from the sea coasts inland to the rural population, who used salt in large quantities for preserving food. This salt was produced by evaporating seawater in pans, relying on the wind and the sun, but sometimes the process was accelerated by the use of wood, peat or coal fires, thus finding two-way burdens for the salters' gals. With the opening of the Cheshire salt mines in Saxon times, the tedious production of sea salt was eclipsed and the packhorse traffic diverted to the saltways from the Cheshire wiches. It is still rewarding to trace the old routes from saltpans on Morecambe Bay and on the Cumbrian shore, such as those over Bleasdale, the Trough of Bowland and Salter Fell. The ways from Cheshire, which proliferated during the agricultural and industrial revolutions, are too numerous to mention.

The depots to which the salt was delivered for local distribution were called 'salt pies'. There is one such today at Rodmer Clough in the Upper Colden valley, now sparsely populated but, according to the census, having five hundred inhabitants, including farmers and handloom weavers, in 1851.

David Hey believes that the buildings named Salt Pie acquired this name because their shape was like a salt box. However, I contend that they did not look any different from the traditional buildings in the countryside, and, if they had, the owner would not have wanted a derogatory name to be perpetuated down the years. But if the name signified the business carried on at that building it would be to the occupier's advantage to have his trade denoted by the name of his establishment, and the quainter the name the better.

In a few instances 'salt' is spelled with a 'p', such as the Psalters Lane into Sheffield. This spelling harks back to monastic days and this explanation of its origin has been perpetuated in modern times, whether genuine or imaginary.

SALT PIE, RODMER CLOUGH, COLDEN

DHOUL'S OR DEVIL'S PAVEMENT, BLACKSTONE EDGE, AS IT IS NOW *(above)* AND SOME FIFTY YEARS AGO *(opposite)*

During the above-mentioned revolutions lime was required in great quantities in the West Riding and East Lancashire textile manufactories, and it had all to be transported by packhorse, most of it over the Pennine hills. The main sources were Clitheroe's, Lothersdale's and Embsay's limestone crags.

Packhorse carriage was so expensive that entrepreneurs found it economic to recover and burn limestone pebbles deposited in the glacial moraine in the valleys to the northeast of Burnley, Nelson and Colne, thus reducing the distance to the West Riding by some 10-12 miles. It is a delightful study today to work out over the ground the various routes taken for delivery of the burnt limestone from these diverse sources to equally diverse destinations in Yorkshire. On these routes will be found the bridges, causeways, waymarkers and holloways described in earlier chapters.

Superstition played a considerable part in the naming of peculiar features which an uneducated population found difficult to understand. Their creation was attributed to the Devil, who was supposed to have made them in a mood of playfulness. Thus we have Devil's pavements, Devil's bridges, Devil's dykes and, of course, the remarkable standing stones called the Devil's Arrows. In mountainous regions there are Devil's kitchens and Devil's punchbowls. The name Dhoul's Pavement on Blackstone Edge is probably a scribe's phonetic transcription of the local country pronunciation of 'devil', and in some sources this stretch is actually called Devil's Pavement.

The woollen textile industry on both sides of the Pennines generated a large amount of packhorse carriage, for raw wool, yarns and woven pieces. The centres for this trade were the cloth halls, initially of Heptonstall, Colne and Rochdale, and later the magnificent structure of Halifax's Piece Hall. Clothiers based here had gangs of horses delivering yarns and collecting pieces from as far away as the farmer-weavers of the Ribble valley. Strangely, this extensive business all over East Lancashire and the West Riding did not name packhorse routes to the same extent as the lime and salt trades, yet the routes to the cloth halls were equally numerous and perhaps of greater economic significance to the industrial revolution.

Chapter 12 The South Pennine Packhorse Trails Trust

Sparked off by the television coverage of events such as the Badminton Horse Trials and the Horse of the Year Show, there was a great upsurge in horseriding in the 1960s. This was the era of Pat Smythe, Harvey Smith's V sign, Princess Anne cursing press photographers and riding for Britain. It was Harold Macmillan's time of 'never had it so good'.

Local riding clubs were formed to organize gymkhanas and shows, tack shops opened for the sale of everything from harness to riding gear, and groups of riders invaded the countryside. It was mainly teenage girls who badgered their parents into buying them a pony, until one-upmanship prevailed and nothing less than a 16-hand hack or hunter would satisfy these horse-mad youngsters, regardless of the cost of its upkeep, which soon turned parents' hair grey.

There was a brief heyday of riders singly or in groups seeking out every cart track or footpath in their district which could be ridden regardless of its status. However, a number of factors combined to threaten this Elysium of freedom. The National Parks and Access to the Countryside Act of 1949, which had been passed with the intention of safeguarding public rights of way by legally recording them at their proper status, had been so poorly implemented that it had created a future timebomb, which would start to explode with the increasing urbanization of the countryside in the second half of the twentieth century. As the old-timers died, the old ways (literally) were forgotten, and a new generation took their place, some of whom wanted to pull up the drawbridge and repell invaders, particularly of the mounted variety.

Landowners were panicked into realizing that, unless they acted, their estates would become a free-for-all not only of sedate middle-aged riders, but, as they imagined, hordes of screaming girls galloping wherever they wanted and, worst of all, young men on trial motorbikes penetrating wherever two wheels could go, even to the mountain tops. The result, following the advice of land agents, was 'Private' notices and locked gates by the hundreds. The riders were effectively excluded from the countryside except on definitive bridleways and, because of the economic depression and deprivation of the first half of the twentieth century, bridleways as a recreational facility had more or less been forgotten through lack of use.

However, in the sixties riding on country lanes and even main roads was reasonably safe with few cars on the road and those of only sedate performance. But increasing affluence brought with it burgeoning car ownership, and one-upmanship again dictated that each succeeding model should have higher speed and acceleration capabilities. Horseriding on motor roads became an unacceptable hazard, and there were hardly any alternatives.

The National Parks and Access to the Countryside Act had stipulated that every county council should draw up a 'definitive map' upon which all the public paths, i.e. 'footpath' or 'bridleway', plus all the minor roads that were mainly used as footpaths and bridleways ('roads used as public paths' or 'RUPPs' as they were called) were to be shown. Once ratified, the definitive map would be conclusive evidence of the existence of public rights of way. However, these maps were prepared for the counties by district and parish councils whose officers and members sometimes had little knowledge of the subject in the field and were not alway prepared to walk the whole district and make exhaustive inquiries into the past and present use of all the footpaths, bridleways and rural roads. In addition, the scale of the survey and the length of time it took to publish the definitive map had been grossly underestimated by government. Indeed, in some counties the definitive map was not published until the 1980s.

Another unforeseen factor bedevilled the situation. The 1949 Act stated that once public paths were recorded on the definitive map, they had to be kept in repair by the highway authorities. County councils such as the West Riding viewed this with dismay, for in certain districts there were hundreds of ancient walled lanes which, if they had to be repaired over their full width as bridleways or RUPPs, would be a highly expensive liability. The simple solution was to record them as 4-foot wide footpaths, a much cheaper item to maintain. In one district alone – Ripponden – out of 93 bridleroads and RUPPs recorded on the draft map, only two survived as bridleways on the definitive version. In the West Riding as a whole some 3,500 RUPPs were quietly demoted to footpath status. This mass downgrading was done without carrying out all the due procedures and without public knowledge, and was totally against the spirit of the 1949 Act. This explains why today many districts such as Cowling which were formerly part of the West Riding have no definitive bridleways at all.

Consequently, the definitive map as published and adopted was full of errors and omissions and, as mentioned earlier, gave every landowner the opportunity to declare private and to close ancient rights of way simply because they were not shown on the map. To compound the problem, it had been enacted that the map should be the *status quo* for five years, when it would be reviewed and amended. This meant that individual errors could not be corrected, but had to wait for the review of the whole map to be carried out. It also became apparent that the period of five years was not sufficient for the review, an unsatisfactory state of affairs where the most serious of errors and omissions had been legalized. So in 1981 a further Act, the Wildlife and Countryside Act, abandoned the five-year review procedure in favour of the principle of continuous review. This meant that routes could be investigated on an individual basis, and if the rights could be substantiated the map would be modified to show them. It became possible for any member of the public to apply to the local highway authority (either a county or a metropolitan council) for a modification order to amend the definitive map to show a particular path at the correct status.

Unfortunately, the procedure that has to be followed is extremely involved, and what starts out as an apparently simple task often turns out to be horrendously complex. The usual reason for applying for a modification order is that a well-used path is suddenly obstructed, often coinciding with a change in ownership of the land crossed by the route. Any public-spirited person can collect a number of evidence forms from people who have used the path in question – in law uninterrupted use by the public for 20 years is conclusive evidence of a public right of way. The next step is a little more difficult: all the landowners and occupiers affected by the path have to be traced and notice served on them. Once this is done, the applicant can apply to the highway authority for a modification order to amend the map.

There the matter rests, sometimes for several years, with the application languishing on an officer's desk in the town hall because public rights of way are not always given a high priority in local government. Eventually the file is opened and the evidence assessed. If the council decides that the evidence is sufficient to suggest that a public right of way exists that has not been recorded, it must make an order to amend the map. However, if any objections are made, usually by the landowners affected, but in the case of a claim for a bridleway ramblers will sometimes object, the whole claim has to be referred to the Secretary of State for the Environment, who usually decides that the matter must be fully aired in front of an independent inspector at a local public inquiry. It can take several

more years to get to this stage.

The public inquiry itself can turn into a nightmare for those who have claimed to have used the path in good faith. The order has to be promoted by the council, calling the applicant and the users as witnesses. Ranged against them are the objectors, often represented by a barrister, who can often demolish the council's case by cross-questioning the witnesses to destroy their credibility and by arguing subtle points of law. Once the public inquiry is finished, and it can last for several days, the inspector then has to write his decision letter giving his reasons for either confirming or rejecting the order.

In the case of a footpath, it is usually fairly easy to find people who have walked the way. However, in the case of a bridleway, horseriders are much thinner on the ground, so collecting user evidence covering a period of 20 years can be extremely problematical. In addition, many old bridleways have been obstructed for years, and as time goes on it becomes increasingly difficult to find people who have ridden them in the past. This task becomes impossible as elderly witnesses die. The most fiercely contested claims are those for 'byway open to all traffic' (a term introduced by the 1968 Countryside Act), with objectors coming out of the woodwork in droves imagining invasion by motorbikes and four-wheel drives.

Another drawback is that the procedure only corrects the definitive map in a piecemeal way. In many areas whole networks of bridleways failed to be recorded. The result is that dedicated horseriders are virtually restricted to riding on busy motor roads. Inevitably there are accidents, sometimes resulting in riders and horses being injured or killed.

SUE HOGG ON INCHFIELD PASTURE CAUSEWAY – ONE OF THE MANY OLD ROADS NOW RECORDED AS FOOTPATHS

A few serious-minded and dedicated individuals searched for a solution, looking particularly at the old packhorse tracks, which were clearly bridleways with use established over hundreds of years. Because of the difficulty of finding user evidence, particularly where an old track has been obstructed for perhaps a hundred years, the alternative is to look for historical evidence and apply for a modification order based on old documents. The application procedure is the same, but theoretically well-researched historical documentary evidence is less easy to challenge at a public inquiry. Unfortunately, many highway authorities do not understand the significance of historical evidence and have to be educated in the history of highways. Some show a remarkable resistance.

Nevertheless, in 1985 Sue Hogg, who lived in Mankinholes, near Todmorden, decided that something had to be done seriously and in depth. The first task was to identify all the main packhorse trails, and she concentrated on the heart of the South Pennines, the area between Burnley, Rochdale and Halifax, where many ancient causeways have survived. By marking on a map all the stretches of causeway, the packhorse bridges, the fords, the wayside guide stoops and crosses marking the junctions of routes, she was able to identify the course of many of the old tracks. Checking the definitive map, she found that the majority of them were either not recorded or only shown as footpaths. So the next stage was to go into the local libraries and archives to look for historical evidence about the tracks and their use.

Because they were the principal highways of their day, the packhorse tracks had to be maintained by the highway surveyors of the parishes or townships through which they passed. The old surveyors kept records of their expenditure, and frequently named the trails they were mending; thus highway surveyors' records proved a very fruitful source of evidence. These were not the only records, however. For example, when a railway or a reservoir was proposed, plans showing the intended work had to be drawn up on which every highway affected by the work was identified and its status recorded. And from the middle of the eighteenth century all the main counties were mapped to show the growing network of turnpike roads with the cross roads running between them. From the same period, many landowners had plans made of their estates, showing the rights of way. Then, of course, there were the inclosure awards and plans, a very important source of evidence, plus the

Quarter Sessions highway orders for repair or removal of obstructions from the highway. Gradually it was possible to assemble a whole series of documents relating to a particular track or series of tracks, as they are all interlinked. This information was then submitted to the local authority as applications for orders to amend the definitive map to show the trails at their correct status.

Digging around in libraries and archives is a time-consuming and costly business. The national records (for turnpikes, reservoirs, railways and the like) are in London, in the House of Lords Record Office and the Public Record Office at Kew, while the county records are kept at the county record offices in Preston, Manchester, Wakefield and Northallerton. It soon became apparent that the task of collecting evidence was so large it could only be tackled in a concerted way. Researching the packhorse trails was a full-time occupation, and as such it needed to be funded.

Meanwhile just across the county boundary in Lancashire, Mary Towneley, an international endurance rider and wife of the Lord Lieutenant of Lancashire, was already campaigning for the preservation of historic tracks in the north of England. In 1986, with two companions, she set out to ride down the spine of England following the old packhorse trails and drovers' roads to publicize the importance of these ancient routes. This ride was the origin of the Pennine Bridleway, the first national trail specifically created for horseriders, which is, at time of writing, being implemented by the Countryside Agency.

Inevitably Mary and Sue got to know each other and, with the encouragement of Tony Greenwood, a

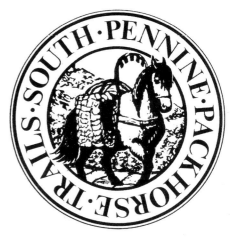

THE TRUST'S LOGO

local schoolteacher and member of Todmorden Town Council, in 1989 they set up the Packhorse Trails Project, with headquarters at The Barn, Mankinholes. A year later this became the South Pennine Packhorse Trails Trust, with Mary and Tony as trustees and Sue as the Trust's paid research officer. With help and funding from UK2000, the Rural Development Commission, the Countryside Commission, the Sports Council and the Standing Conference of South Pennine Authorities, and with the support of the British Horse Society, the Trust embarked on a concerted programme of research with the aim of getting the packhorse tracks properly recorded on the definitive map.

In order to carry out its work, the Trust depends heavily on information and help from a whole variety of voluntary workers – horseriders, local historians, ramblers, cyclists, motorbikers and 4-wheel drivers. Interest in the Trust's work is not just confined to

RESTORING THE PACKHORSE TRAILS IS HEAVY WORK

(above) REBUILDING THE FORD AT TURNHOLE CLOUGH, TRAWDEN

(top right) REMOVING AN OBSTRUCTION WHILE RESTORING HEIGHTS ROAD, RIPPONDEN

(bottom right) STONEPITCHING ON STANDEDGE

GISBURN OLD ROAD BEFORE *(above)* AND AFTER RESTORATION *(below)*

totalling 90 km of bridleways and byways, with another 20 claims waiting to be determined. Since 1989 it has raised over £570,000, which has been spent on research for modification order applications and on repairing routes once they have been accepted as bridleways.

The repair work followed on naturally from getting the status of the tracks sorted out. Minor work, such as cutting back overgrown vegetation, can be done by volunteer work parties. The Trust itself concentrates on major repairs such as drainage and surfacing, with the work done by a professional contractor who has machines suitable for working in confined spaces and on soft ground. The aim is to restore the trails in keeping with their

horseriders. In 1994 the Trust set up a Supporters' Group and to date this has attracted over two hundred members and has raised over £7000 towards the Trust's work.

All the information collected over the years has to be stored somewhere, and to this end The Barn has been commandeered, not only as the Trust's headquarters, but as a mini reference library for all the source material gathered in the course of making claims. A computer enables Sue to produce newsletters, pamphlets and guides, as well as keeping a track of all the applications.

From its first beginnings the Trust has helped to recover over 53 trails,

original character, using local sandstone wherever possible. The result is the restoration of a long-neglected feature of our countryside with the consequent enhancement of the wild beauty of the moorlands. To date the Trust has improved 45 routes (90 km), including 20 for which it had obtained definitive status; it also works on existing bridleways for local councils. Currently (2002) it is working on sections of the Mary Towneley Loop, a 42-mile circular route forming part of the Pennine Bridleway, named after the person who worked so hard both for the Trust and for the national trail, but sadly died before the latter was completed.

The Trust operates on the basis of the three Rs: research, restoration and recreation. Defined and restored, the packhorse trails are there for the public to enjoy, an important leisure facility and potentially a unique tourism attraction which is part and parcel of the South Pennine landscape. To achieve this, the next step in the Trust's activities was to produce map guides to the routes. The first guidebook, for a 45-mile route from Marsden and Delph to Haworth and Oxenhope, was published in 1997, and two further guides are in the pipeline. They have been specifically designed for horse riders: for example, they show water troughs and the different types of surface to be encountered, including boggy ground. At the same time they can be used by mountain-bikers and walkers who want to explore the uplands following historic routes. All the surveying work and mapping has been done by two volunteers, John Presgrave and John B. Taylor, who have spent countless hours walking and sketching the trails.

One of the Trust's major achievements came in 1996, when it was awarded a lottery grant towards a three-year programme of research and restoration to create the South Pennine bridleways network. This was the first project of its kind to receive lottery funding, and set a national precedent by establishing that research to obtain definitive status to enable the creation of a recreational facility is eligible for lottery funding.

The Trust's main work – the recording of historic routes – acquired particular importance in December 2000. The Countryside and Rights of Way Act, which brought in the right to roam for people on foot, has also introduce legislation to extinguish historic rights of way if by the year 2026 they are not recorded on the definitive map. So if an ancient bridleroad is only shown as a footpath and has fallen out of use by horses, the bridleway rights will disappear in 2026 unless they can be claimed before the cut-off date. The same applies to vehicular rights. Incredibly, the CROW Act has overturned the age-old principle of 'once a highway, always a highway'. Just to make matters more confusing, where a vehicular right of way is not recorded on the definitive map, the rights will remain, but after 2026 they cannot be added to the definitive map.

Many people feel that our higher rights of way have been sacrificed to the interests of a vocal minority of ramblers, who, although they already have an extensive network of footpaths (and bridleways and byways come to that) across the country, also demanded a right to roam. The promise to extinguish the public's rights in 2026 was offered by the Government as the *quid pro quo* to landowners faced with open access. In this trade-off, the greatest losers will be horse riders, although countless other users will also be seriously affected.

So in the twenty-first century much of our amazing heritage of ancient tracks is in danger of being lost to private interests. Throughout the country there are thousands of old drove roads, packhorse tracks and bridleways now under threat of extinction. To research and record them all will be an impossible task, and there are only a few people able and willing to take it on. The Trust's work is even more vital now in what has become a race against time.

Glossary

abutment: the structure that supports the arch of a bridge

alle, alley: a road or way, from the French *aller* ('to go'); hence Allescholes

badger: a licensed travelling seller; hence Badger Lane, Badgergate

baiting: a stopping place for food or rest ('bait'); hence Baitings Inn

blackgate, blackway: a track crossing peaty ground

brink: a short steep slope or drop

broadgate: a wide walled way

cairn: a pile of stones used as a waymarker

cantilever bridge: a bridge constructed from two large, upward sloping flagstones with another long flagstone placed across them to bridge the gap

carrier: a person who operates packhorse trains

cascade: a series of man-made steps constructed down a watercourse to regulate its violence

cateran: a Scottish drover, sometimes modified to 'Catherine', e.g. Catherine House and Catherine Lane, Luddenden

catt: a naturally occuring aggregate compounded of clay, silt, marl and gravel, used extensively in early farmhouses, being beaten down for flooring in both house and farm buildings. Also used as the foundation for elevated causeways. Hence placenames such as Cattholes, Cattridge and Catt-steps

caul: a curved dam or weir (from 'caul' = curved head-dress)

causeway: from the Old French *caucie*, a paved or raised way

causey: a line of stone paving; a causeway stone; also variant of 'causeway' (see above)

chapman: a travelling trader

clam bridge: a bridge made of a huge slab of stone laid across a stream

clapper bridge: a bridge made of strong flagstones laid on pillars that rise from the stream or river bed

clough: a steep inclined valley often with a stream. The word refers to the land formation not the water

clunter: (1) a rocky, rugged precipice often with loose rocks; (2) a clod of earth; (3) a tussock of grass, usually tufted purple molinia

coolam: an area of land under which there are coal seams

cote: (1) a small inclosure, sometimes with a shelter,

used for packhorses, e.g. saddling cote; (2) a primitive cottage or house

culvert: a covered stone channel built to carry water under a road

cut: a trackway excavated across an area of clunters (see above)

cutwater: the wedge-shaped end of a pier of a bridge which serves to divide the current, break up ice, etc.

ding/dingle: a ravine or small valley

drift: (a) a type of coalmine entered by an inclined passage; (b) a natural deposit of coal

driftway: a road used for driving cattle

drove road: long-distance route for driving cattle

edgeway: a track that goes along a solid edge of a hill to avoid boggy ground

finger post: a guide post with the direction indicated by a pointing finger

ford: a crossing point on a river or stream where the water is shallow enough to pass through on foot or on hoof

gait: a style of walking; *see also* **gate**

gaiters: leg protectors, usually made of polished leather

gal or galloway: a type of small horse used for pack carrying, originating from the Galloway area of Scotland. The breed is now extinct

gate (gait): from the Old Norse *gata*, meaning a road or a journey

ginnel: a narrow, walled snicket (see below)

grip: a man-made ditch or trench

gudgeon: an iron fitting on a gate for hanging it on a gatestoop. The gudgeon fits over the gudgeon pin or pintle to form a hinge

guide, guide stoop: a stone post erected at a junction of tracks as a waymarker

hag or hagg: a copse or coppice

haigh/hay: (1) originally an inclosed field; subsequently a pasture or a homestead; (2) a hedgerow

hebble: a plank foot-bridge

heck/heckle: a gate or the lower part of a split farm door

hey: land enclosed by walls or hedges

hog's back: see **humpbacked bridge**

holloway: a route which has been dug out or worn down so that it runs as a deep cutting between high banks

humpbacked bridge: a bridge whose surface arches over a stream; sometimes called a hog's back

hushing: an artificial stream created to extract lime deposits by washing away the soil

ing: (1) a watermeadow; (2) a hill or peak

jag: a load (dialect)

jagger, jaggerman: a packhorse driver

jumb: a deep pool in a river

keld: a well or spring on a slope; a slope with a well or spring on it

keystone: the central stone at the top an arch which locks the whole structure together

knoll/knowl: a hilltop or hill

knott: rocky or peaked projection on a mountainside

lumb: a pool or grove; derived from 'lum' meaning a deep hole or a small wood

menhir: a large standing stone possibly used for religious ceremonies or as a waymarker

mistal: a cowhouse

moor-fence track: a track running along the edge of a moor following an inclosure wall or fence

moorgate: a walled track leading onto unenclosed land (moor or common)

moss: an expanse of wet peat

narrowgate: a narrow walled way

naze: a projecting ridge or headland (like a nose)

owler: (1) a wool smuggler; (2) an elder tree

ox wain: a cart drawn by oxen

pack and prime way: a highway for use on foot or on horseback, hence a bridleway or driftway. '. . . it is both a footway, which was the first, or *primeway*, and a *pack* or *driftway* also' (Lord Coke)

pinder: a man who looks after a pinfold

pinfold: an enclosure for stray stock

pintle: an iron pin attached to a gatestoop for hanging a gate (see **gudgeon**)

plinth: (1) the base of a pier of a bridge; (2) the projecting part of wall immediately above the ground

pound: an enclosure for stray animals

rake: a track running at an angle across the face of a hill

ridgeway: a route running along the ridge of a hill

roger: a rogue, hence 'Roger Pasture' = dangerous ground

saddle bridge: a humpbacked bridge with parapets, giving the appearance of a packsaddle

saddling cote: see **cote**

salt pie: a building used as a depot for salt

scout: a high rock, projecting ridge or overhanging rock

sett: a cut stone block used for paving a road

shaw or shay: a wooded valley, small group of trees, copse or thicket

shippen, shippon: a cowhouse

slab bridge: see **clam bridge**

snicket: (1) a narrow passageway between buildings; (2) a narrow gate

spandrels: stone ribs used to strengthen a bridge

spitalfield: a field used for overnight grazing, from 'hospital'

spate: fast-flowing floodwater

staircase/stairs: a steep track, often stepped

stang: a pole used for fitting into slots in stone gate stoops

swaler/swailer: a wholesale dealer in corn and provisions, from 'swale' = a large, coarse basket

stoop: a stone post, as in guide stoop, gate stoop

teamster: a packhorse driver

tenter: to stretch; hence 'tenterhooks' = hooks used for stretching cloth

thrang: busy and crowded

tump: a small prominence used as a sighting point

turnbye: a stone kerb running diagonally across a

road to direct water off the surface and into roadside drains

turnpike: an improved road for use by carriages upon the payment of a toll; such roads were administered by a trust

turves: peat sods cut for drying and burning

wain: a single-axled farm cart, approximately 4 feet wide

waingate/wainsgate: a waggon road

wham: (1) bog, marsh or swamp; (2) a large drainage ditch

wich: from the Old English *wic*, meaning a shed or building used for drying salt; hence a place where there are brine pits, as in Northwich

whitegate, whiteway: a track crossing ground covered in bent grass

will: a willow tree; hence 'will-ing', a meadow with willows, as in Willing Wham

windy harbour: an overnight stopping place or shelter for cattle or packhorses

Further Reading

Bernard Barnes, *Passages Through Time: Saddleworth roads and trackways*, Saddleworth Historical Society, 1981

K. J. Bonser, *The Drovers*, Country Book Club, 1972

Herbert C. Collins, *The Roof of Lancashire,* Dent, 1950

W. B. Crump, 'Ancient Highways of the Parish of Halifax', a series of nine papers published in the *Transactions of the Halifax Antiquarian Society*, 1924-27

W. B. Crump, *Huddersfield Highways down the Ages*, 1949; republished in facsimile by Kirklees Leisure Services, 1988

W. B. Crump, 'Saltways of the Cheshire Wiches', *Transactions of the Lancashire and Cheshire Antiquarian Society*, vol. 54, 1936, pp. 84-142

David Hey, *Packmen, Carriers and Packhorse Roads: trade and communications in North Derbyshire and South Yorkshire*, Leicester University Press, 1980

Ernest Hinchliffe, *A Guide to the Packhorse Bridges of England*, Cicerone Press, 1944

James Maxim, *A Lancashire Lion*, Trustees of the Estate of the Late James Maxim, 1965

James Maxim, 'Packhorse and Other Ancient Tracks', *Transactions of the Rochdale Literary and Scientific Society*, 25 February 1927, vols. 16-18, 1926-34

Arthur Raistrick, *Green Roads in the Mid-Pennines*, Moorland Publishing, 1991

Titus Thornber, *A Pennine Parish: the history of Cliviger*, Rieve Edge Press, Briercliffe, Burnley, 1987

Sidney and Beatrice Webb, *The Story of the King's Highway*, 1913; republished by Frank Cass, 1963 (English Local Government Series, vol. 5)

Geoffrey N. Wright, *Roads and Trackways of the Yorkshire Dales*, Moorland Publishing, 1991

Gazetteer

Grid references carry the prefix SD, unless another prefix is included. The majority of locations can be found on OS Outdoor Leisure map no. 21 (South Pennines), and its successor OS Explorer OL21.

Allescholes milestone 941 202
Baitings Gate 001 187
Bashall Brook saddle bridge 702 435
Bearnshaw Tower 904 258
Beaumont Clough Road, Erringden 980 261–982 267
Beaver Cote, Boulsworth 933 372
Beckfoot bridge SE 105 384
Bell House, Erringden 996 246
Bell House Moor, Erringden 99 24
Beverley Bank, Jumble Hole Clough 96 26
Black Hameldon, Cliviger 91 29
Blackshaw Head 96 27
Blackstone Edge causeway 962 168–989 184
Blue Bell Lane, Shore-in-Stansfield 913 268–921 266
Bottomley, Walsden 942 211
Boulsworth Hill, Trawden 93 36
Bridgeley Bank, Dunnockshaw 82 28
Brink Ends Farm, Boulsworth 942 379
Brontë Falls 998 358
Browsholme Hall 685 454
Buttress, Hebden Bridge 992 272–990 276
Causeway House, Cliviger 887 293
Causeway Wood, Todmorden 95 23
Chapel House, Hebden Bridge 990 277
Chatburn 76 44
Clunters 943 270

Cock Hill SE 01 32
Colden 96 28
Coombe Hill Cross, Trawden 955 385
Cornholme, Todmorden 91 26
Cowling 97 43
Cowpe 82 20
Cragg Vale SE 00 23
Cranberry Dam, White Slack Gate 925 205
Cromwell's Bridge 704 391
Crook Moor, Wardle 91 19
Crowbrook (Paul Clough) 909 279
Dark Lane, Rodmer Clough 954 288–952 291
Dhoul's Pavement, Blackstone Edge 986 180–987 183
Draughton milestone SE 039 511
Duke's Cross (site of), Burnley–Halifax Long Causeway 898 286
Duke's Cut, Blackshaw Head 935 273–938 286
Dunnockshaw 81 27
Earnshaw Water culvert, Blackshaw Head 948 275
Eastwood Road, Blackshaw Head 932 273–960 262
Float (Flout) Bridge, Trawden 897 367
Foster Bridge, Hebden Bridge 991 278
Four Gates End, Duke's Cut, Blackshaw Head 938 286
Gambleside village (site of), Dunnockshaw 83 28
Gauxholme 92 23
Gilford Clough ford, Trawden 920 371
Gisburn Old Road 870 425–828 480
Gorple 918 320
Gorple stream ford 948 315
Graining Water, Widdop 95 31
Hameldon Hill, Dunnockshaw 81 28

Hapton High Park 81 28
Hardcastle Craggs 98 29
Harden Brook, Bingley SE 10 38
Harley Wood Gate, Blackshaw Head 952 274
Hippins Clough, Blackshaw Head 95 27
Hartley Royd, Shore-in-Stansfield 918 266
Haworth SE 03 37
Hebble End, Hebden Bridge 989 272
Hebble Hole clam bridge, Colden 965 281
Hebden Bridge packhorse bridge 992 273
Hebden Hey, Hardcastle Craggs 978 291
Heights Road, Ripponden SE 044 194–046 196
Hellyplatt, Cliviger 876 290
Heptonstall Moor 93 30
Heptonstall Slack 97 28
Herders' Inn, Trawden 945 391
Herders' Rake, Cliviger 895 267–902 269
High Withens (Top Withens, Wuthering Heights) 981 354
Hippins bridge, Blackshaw Head 958 271
Hippins Clough bridge, Blackshaw Head 947 272
Hodder bridge *see* Cromwell's Bridge
Hollingworth Lane, Walsden 942 211–939 217
Horsehold, Hebden Bridge 983 267
Hudson Moor, Stansfield 92 26
Hudson Moor causeway, Stansfield 921 266–924 265
Hurstwood, Cliviger 88 31
Inchfield 92 21
Inchfield Pasture 91 22
Inchfield Pasture causeway 922 220–924 226
Ings Beck bridge, Chatburn 785 454
Issues Road, Holme SE 086 055–104 063
Jack Bridge, Colden 962 282
Jumble Hole Clough bridge 963 267
Kennel Lane, Oxenhope SE 013 345–018 343
Limers' (Limey) Lane, Gambleside 83 28
Limersgate, via Brown Wardle 897 162–892 176–896 186–902 198–902 206–901 220–890 241
Limersgate, via Cock Hill 999 310–SE 025 280 025

Littleborough 94 16
London Road, Langfield Common 960 234–984 250
Long Causeway (Burnley–Halifax) 874 306–958 276
Long Causeway (Stoodley Long Causeway), Langfield Common 957 233–958 233
Long Stoop, Langfield Common 968 231
Lower Allescholes 935 207
Lower Hodder bridge *see* Cromwell's bridge
Lower Rawtonstall, Hebden Bridge 977 273
Luddenden Dean SE 03 27
Lumb Falls bridge, Hardcastle Craggs 992 314
Lumb Stairs, Hardcastle Craggs 992 313–995 313
Lumbutts 95 23
Lumbutts Lane 956 235–959 237
Magna Via, Halifax SE 101 254–117 252
Maiden Cross (site of), Burnley–Halifax Long Causeway 894 288
Malham clapper bridge 900 630
Mankinholes 96 23
Marsden, Lancashire 86 36
Mereclough, Cliviger 87 30
Moorbottom Road, Boulsworth Hill 902 361–955 385
Moorcock Road, Blackshaw Head 939 286–947 279
Mount Cross, Shore-in-Stansfield 915 273
Mytholm 98 27
Naze Road, Gauxholme 925 227–929 231
Newsholme Dean cantilever bridge SE 022 395
Noahdale Road, Blackshaw Head 935 291–939 286
North Hollingworth, Walsden 939 217
Northwell Lane, Heptonstall 987 281–988 290
Old Chamber, Hebden Bridge 99 26
Old Scotch Road, Boulsworth Hill 90 35
Ox Lee Lane, Hepworth SE 159 058–175 052
Paul Clough bridge, Cornholme 906 271
Pot Oven Farm, Cliviger 879 280
Public Slake Trough, Langfield Common 976 242
Pule and Standish common SE 02 10
Ragby bridge, Inchfield 922 215
Raistrick Greave, Widdop 932 309

Rake End, Salter Rake Gate 939 227
Ramsden Long Causeway 922 212
Reaps Cross, Heptonstall Moor 944 302
Red Moss, Cliviger 84 27
Reddyshore Scout Gate 944 190–941 202
Ridge Gate, Shore-in-Stansfield 914 268–921 266
Robin Cross (site of), Burnley–Halifax Long Causeway
  881 297
Rodmer Clough, Upper Colden 96 29
'Roman Road', Blackstone Edge 962 168–975 172
Rooley Moor Road 871 159–848 219
Rough Hill 91 20
Rough Hill causeway 914 200–910 208
Rush Candle Clough, Black Hameldon 92 29
Salter Rake Gate, Lumbutts 939 217–946 231
Shedden bridge, Cliviger 891 301
Shedden Drove Road (Worsthorne Road), Cliviger 893
  294–894 298
Shepherd's Rest, Lumbutts 945 232
Shurcrack milestone, Lumbutts 944 230
Slack Chapel, Heptonstall 977 287
Sourhall, Todmorden 917 247
South Hollingworth, Walsden 939 215
Sowerby SE 04 23
Standedge SE 01 09
Standing Stone Height, Cliviger 91 32
Stones, Todmorden 925 235
Staups Moor, Blackshaw Head 95 26
Stiperden 90 27
Stiperden Cross (site of), Burnley–Halifax Long Causeway
  904 283
Stones, Todmorden 925 235
Stoodley Long Causeway 957 233–958 233
Stoodley Pike 972 242
Stump Cross (site of), Burnley–Halifax Long Causeway
  878 300

Thursden 904 349
Todmorden Edge 923 245
Top Brink milestone, Lumbutts 957 235
Top of Stairs, Oxenhope Moor SE 003 337
Top Withens 981 354
Tower Causeway, Todmorden 911 251–904 258
Turnhole Clough ford, Trawden 940 379
Upper Gorple reservoir 92 31
Waddington 72 44
Walsden 93 22
Warland 94 20
Watergrove village (site of) 91 18
Watersheddles Cross 971 382
Watty Lane, Gauxholme 929 231–925 235
Weasel Hall, Erringden 991 264
Whirlaw, Stansfield 93 25
White Slack Gate 920 201–935 208
  standing stone 932 208
Widdop Gate 966 311
Widdop Head 915 335
Windgate Nick, Addingham SE 069 471
Windy Harbour, Stansfield 937 261
Windy Harbour, Cliviger 876 290
Withens, Erringden 98 23
Withens Gate, Langfield Common 969 231
Worsthorne 87 32
Worthorne Road, Cliviger 89 29
Wuthering Heights 982 355
Wycoller old causeway 955 385–971 382
Wycoller 93 39
  clam bridge 936 389
  clapper bridge 932 392
  packhorse bridge 932 392

Index

Page numbers of illustrations are shown in bold type.

A
abutments, 14, 17
Acts of Parliament
  Blackstone Edge Turnpike Act (1734), xvii
  Countryside Act (1968), 82
  Countryside and Rights of Way Act (2000), 87
  Elizabeth I (1662), 5
  erection of signposts, 49
  Halifax–Burnley Turnpike Act (1759), 28
  inclosure by, 69
  National Parks and Access to the Countryside Act (1949), 80
  Philip and Mary (1555), 3, 5, 6, 23
  waterworks, 72
  Wildlife and Countryside Act (1981), 81
  see also Statute of Bridges
agricultural revolution, 67
agriculture, decline of, 71
Allescholes, 75
Allescholes milestone, 8, **50**, 51
alley, alleyway, 75
Ancient British, 73
Anglo-Saxon, 73, 75

B
Baitings Gate, 66
Bakewell Bridge, 15
balance beam, 57
Bannockburn, 17
Bashall Brook saddle bridge, 11, **11**
beacons, 52
Bearnshaw Tower, 65
Beaumont Clough Road, Horsehold, **56**
Beaver Cote, Boulsworth, 66
Beckfoot bridge, 16
Bell House, 64
Bell House Moor, Erringden, xviii, 64
bell mare, 32
bent grass, 27
Beverley Bank, Jumble Hole Clough, 19
Bewick, Thomas, xx
Black Hameldon, 44
Blackshaw Head, 17, 23, 28
Blackstone Edge, 31, 32, 45
  causeway, xv
Blackwell Hall, London, xvi
Bleasdale, saltways, 77
Blue Bell Lane, Shore-in-Stansfield, 66
Bonny Prince Charlie, 31
Boroughbridge, 17, 46

Bottomley, Walsden, 38, 59
Boulsworth Hill, 25, 43, 58, 66
boundary mounds, 43
Bridgeley Bank, Dunnockshaw, 34, **34**, 51
bridges
  abutments, 14, 17
  arched, 9-17
    construction, **12**, 13
  Bakewell, 15
  Bashall Brook, 11
  Beckfoot, 16
  cantilever, 9, 20-21, **21**, 46
  circular, **13**, 14
  clam, 9, 19, **19**, **20**, 46
  clapper, 9, 17, **18**
  Cromwell's, **14**, 17
  cutwaters, 17
  Foster, 15
  Great Haywood, 17
  Hebden, 15
  Hippins Clough, **16**, 17
  hog's back, 10
  humpbacked, 10
  Ings Beck, **10**, 11
  Lumb Falls, 11
  parapets, 10
  Paul Clough, **13**, 14
  Ragby, 29
  railway, Firth of Forth, 20

saddle, 11, **11**
Shedden, 16
slab *see* clam
spandrels, 12
straight-across, 10, 17
Wycoller, 11
bridleway routes, 59
bridleways, 80
Briercliffe, xviii
Brink Ends Farm, Boulsworth, 58
brinks, 37-8, **37**
Britannia, xvii
Britannia Inferior, 1, 2
British Horse Society, 84
broadgates, 6, 31, 58
Brontë Falls, 20, 45
Brontë, Emily, 45
Browsholme Hall, 11
Burnley, xviii, 28, 38, 64, 73, 75, 83
Buttress, Hebden Bridge, 59
bywashes, 60
byways, 75
byways open to all traffic, 82

C
cairns, 53
Calderdale Archives, 31, 48
Cambridgeshire, xv
Canal Mania, 5
canals, 2
cantilever bridge *see* bridges
carriers, xviii-xvxix
cart roads, 60
cascade 24-5, **25**
catt, 30, 40
cattle droving, xv
caul see cascade
Causeway House, Cliviger, 47
causeway placenames, 75
Causeway Wood, Todmorden, 37

causeways, 6
accidents on, 32
Blackstone Edge, xv-xvi
construction, 26, 30-31
floating, 41
gradient of, 29
improved, 31
in South Pennines, 83
in Upper Gorple reservoir, **40**
Inchfield Pasture, **41**
Kennel Lane, Oxenhope, **26**
Long Causeway, Langfield
  Common, 27
lost, 28, 32, 40, **40**
Hudson Moor, Stansfield, **32**
Rough Hill, **39**, 44
Magna Via, Halifax, **28**
North Hollingworth–Lumbutts, 30
raised, **29**, 30
Salter Rake Gate, Lumbutts, **29**
rakes, 30, 31, 38
Ramsden Long Causeway, **42**
setted, 29
shelfway, 30-31, **30**
stepped, 29, 30, 31
water damage, 59
width, 27, 31, 32
Wycoller, **48**
causey, 26
Chapel House finger post, Hebden
  Bridge, 51
Chat Moss, 40
Chatburn, 11
Cheshire, 65
  salt mines, 76
  saltways, 77
Chester, xvi
Civil War, xvi, 48
Clitheroe lime trade, 78
Cliviger, 44, 56
Cliviger Gorge, **3**

Cliviger inclosure road, **70**
cloth halls, xvi, 79
cloth trade, xvi-xvii, **xix**, 79
clunters, 7, 43
Clunters, 43
Clydesdales, xix
Cock Hill, 42
Cock Hill Moor, 29
Colden Water, 19
Colne, 17, 79
common in the soil *see* rights of
  common
common land *see* wastes of the manor
commoners, 67
compounding, 67
Coombe Hill cross, Trawden, **46**
copyhold land, 69
Cornholme, Todmorden, 14
Countryside Act (1968), 82
Countryside Agency, 84
Countryside and Rights of Way Act
  (2000), 87
Countryside Commission, 84
county bridges, 5
county rate, 5
Cowling, 81
Cowpe, 34
Crag Gill, 39
Cragg Vale, 59, 64
Cranberry Dam, White Slack Gate,
  64
Cromwell's Bridge, **14**, 17
Crook Moor, Wardle, 28
cross roads, xvi, 83
crosses, 46
  Celtic, 48
  Coombe Hill, **46**
  Mount, 47
  on Burnley–Halifax Long
    Causeway, 47
  Reaps, 31, **48**

removal of, 48
Watersheddles, **48**
Crowbrook, 24
Crump, W. B., xvi, 65
culverts, 22-3, **23**
Cumbria, saltways, 77
cuts
    Cut, The, 43
    Duke's Cut, 43, 51, **69**
    Eastwood Road, 43
cutwaters, 17

D
Danelaw, 73
Dark Ages, 73
Dark Lane, Rodmer Clough, **35**
Dartmoor ponies, 76
deer leaps, 43
definitive map, 7
    compilation of, 81
    cut-off date, 87
    modification orders, 82
    reviews, 81
definitive status, packhorse tracks, 7
Defoe, Daniel, xiv
Dent, 39
Derbyshire, 15
    saddle bridges in, 11
devil placenames, 79
Devil's Pavement see Dhoul's
    Pavement
Devon, xviii
Devonshire packhorse, xx
Dhoul's Pavement, Blackstone Edge,
    78, 79, **79**
drainage problems, 58
drainage system, Magna Via, Halifax,
    59
Draughton milestone, **51**
drove roads, 6, 58
    and inclosure, 69

drovers, 66, 74
    language of, 75
    stopping places, 52
droving, xv, 36
Duke's Cross, Burnley–Halifax Long
    Causeway, 47
Duke's Cut, Blackshaw Head, 43, 51,
    69
Dunnockshaw, 34

E
Earnshaw Water, Blackshaw Head, 23
East Anglia, xv
East Lancashire, 40
    cloth trade, 79
    limestone deposits, 78
Eastgate, Burnley, 75
Eastwood Road, Blackshaw Head, 43
edgeways, 37-8, **37**, **38**
Elmet, 73
Embsay lime trade, 78
encroachment, 67
English language, 73, 75
erosion, 33
estate records, 83
estovers see rights of comon

F
Farrer family, 59
Fielden, John, 51
finger posts, 50, **51**
fish transport, xviii
Flanders, packhorse trade to, 47
Float (Flout) Bridge, Trawden, xviii
fodder, 40
footbridges, 15, 21
fords, 19, 24
    cascade or caul, **24**, 25, **25**
    Gorple stream, 31
    Turnhole Clough, Trawden, **85**
Foster Bridge, Hebden Bridge, 15

Foul Moss, 40
freehold land, 67
freeholders, 67, 69

G
gal see Galloway
Gallgate, 76
Galloway, xvi, xix-xx, **xix**, 76
Galloway Gate, 76
Galloway roads, 76
Gambleside, Dunnockshaw, 34, 51
gate, meaning of, 75
gates, 54
gatestoops
    with balance beam, 57-8, **57**
    with stang slots, 54-5, **55**
    with square holes, **55**, **56**, 57-8
gateways 56
    with stang poles, **55**
Gauxholme, 29
geese droving, xv, 36
Gilford Clough, Trawden, 25, **25**
ginnels, 58-9, **58**
Gisburn Old Road, **86**
Gorple reservoirs, 40, **40**
Gorple stream, 31
Graining Water, Widdop, **30**, 31
grazing charges, 63
Great Haywood bridge, Staffordshire,
    17
Great North Road, xvi
Greenwood, Tony, 84
Grimes Graves, Norfolk, 37
grooves see hushings
gudgeons, 54, **54**
guideposts, authorized by Justices of
    the Peace, 5
guidestoops
    Allescholes, **50**
    Four Gates End, Blackshaw Head,
    51

in West Riding, 51
Long Stoop, 51
Lumbutts Lane, 37
Shurcrack, **50**
Top Brink, 37, **50**
White Slack Gate, **49**, 51

H
haigh, 53
Halfpenny Lane, Longridge, 63
Halfpenny Pasture, 63
Halifax, 28, 37, 83
Halifax Piece Hall, 79
Hameldon Hill, Dunnockshaw, 34
Hapton High Park, 57
Hardcastle Craggs, 30
Harden Brook, Bingley, 16
Harley Wood Gate, Blackshaw Head,
   16, 17
Hippins Clough, Blackshaw Head,
   16, 17
Hartley Royd, Shore-in-Stansfield, 66
Haworth, 20, 29, 37
Hebble End, Hebden Bridge, xviii,
   37, 59, 64
Hebble Hole clam bridge, Colden,
   20
Hebden Bridge, 15, 17, 37, 43, 51,
   59
Hebden Hey, Hardcastle Craggs, 30
Hebden Water, 15, 17
hedgerows, on rights of way, **52**, 53
Heights Road, Ripponden, **85**
Hellyplatt, Cliviger, 64
Heptonstall, 15, 17, 28, 29, 51, 59
   cloth hall, 79
Heptonstall Moor, 72
Heptonstall Slack, 50
Herders' Inn, Trawden, 58
Herders' Rake, Cliviger, **3**
Hey, David, 11, 77

Heywood, Oliver, 32
High Withens, 53
highway authority, 82
highway orders, 84
highway rate, 4, 5, 70
highway repair, 4-5, 60
highway surveyor, 6, 49, 83
highways, 75
Hippins Bridge, Blackshaw Head, 17
Hippins Clough bridge, Blackshaw
   Head, **16**, 17
Hodder bridge *see* Cromwell's Bridge
Hollingworth Lane, Walsden, **2**
holloways, 31, 33-6
   Bridgeley Bank, Dunnockshaw, 34,
      34
   Dark Lane, Rodmer Clough, **35**
   Holloway, London, **35**, 36
   Limers' Lane, Gambleside, 34
   moor-fence tracks, 71
   Old Scotch Road, Boulsworth, **33**
   Ox Lee Lane, Hepworth, **36**
Holmfirth, 31
horse pastures, 6, 64
Horsehold, Hebden Bridge, **65**
horse-load, xix, 75-6
horseriding, 80
horseway, 70
hospital/hospice, 64
House of Lords Record Office, 84
Huddersfield, xviii, 31
Hudson Moor, Stansfield, lost
   causeway, 32
Hugh of Elland, xv, xvi
Hurstwood, Cliviger, 16
hushings, 33, 43

I
Ice Age, 34
Inchfield, 28
Inchfield Pasture causeway, **41**, **83**

inclosure, 67-9
   effect of, 6, 70
   provision for rights of way, 69
inclosure awards, 69
inclosure maps, **68**, 69
   Cliviger, **70**
   Stansfield, 43, **68**
inclosure commissioner, 69
   powers of, 71
inclosure records, 83
inclosure roads, 70
   Duke's Cut, **69**
   Noahdale Road, **68**
   Shedden Drove Road (Worsthorne
      Road), **70**
Industrial Revolution, 13, 63, 67, 73
   expansion of trade routes, 6
Ingleborough, 59
Ings Beck bridge, Chatburn, **10**, 11
Ireland, xvi
Issues Road, Holme, 7

J
Jack Bridge, Colden, 19
jag, jagger, 75
jagger ponies, **76**
Jumble Hole Clough, 19
Jumble Hole Clough clam bridge, **19**
Justices of the Peace, 5
justices' trusts, 4

K
Kendalmen, xviii
Kennel Lane, Oxenhope, **26**
King's Highway, 1, 3
   and inclosure, 69

L
Lake District, 73
Lancashire, xv, 84
Lancashire and Cheshire Antiquarian

Society, 65
Lancashire–Yorkshire border, 24
Lancaster, 59
land types, 27
landowners, and public rights of way, 82
lanes, 75
Langfield Common, **xix**, **27**, 28, 51
Langfield Edge, 30, 51
Latin, 73
lead mining, 34
leading gudgeons, **54**
lime trade, 78
Limers' Lane, Gambleside, 34
limers' ways
    Burnley–Manchester, 34
    Clitheroe–Rochdale, 34
    on Ordnance Survey maps, 76
Limersgate, Brown Wardle Hill, 72
Limersgate, Cock Hill, 42
limersgates, 8
    Lothersdale–Halifax, 43
    Lothersdale–Saddleworth, xviii
    Lumb Stairs, 29
    Wardle–Sharneyford, 72
limestone deposits, 78
Lincolnshire, 63
Littleborough, xvi, 31
local populations, differences in, 73
London, 84
London Road, Langfield Common, **71**
Long Causeway
    Burnley–Halifax, 19, 23, **23**, 28, 64
        crosses on, 47
        Stiperden, 24
    Langfield Common, **xiv**, **27**
    see also Stoodley Long Causeway
    Lumbutts–Cragg Vale, 28, 37
    Wardle–Watergrove–Inchfield, 28, 29, 31

Long Stoop, Langfield Common, 51
Longridge, 64
Lord of the Manor, 67, 68, 69
Lothersdale, 59
    and lime trade, xviii, 78
Lower Allescholes, 51
Lower Hodder bridge *see* Cromwell's bridge
Lower Rawtonstall, Hebden Bridge, **xv**, 53
Luddenden Dean, 29, 43
Lumb Falls, Hardcastle Craggs, **xiii**, 43
Lumb Stairs, Hardcastle Craggs, 29
Lumbutts, 28, 30, 51
Lumbutts Lane, 37
Lydgate, 54
Lyme Regis, xviii

M
Mace, Thomas, xvii
Magna Via, Halifax, **28**, **59**
Maiden Cross, Burnley–Halifax Long Causeway, 47, 66
Malham, 52
Malham clapper bridge, **18**
Manchester, 84
Mankinholes, 51, 83
    water troughs, **62**
manor court rolls, 69
manorial surveys, 67
maps
    Heptonstall township, 31
    Holloway, London, **35**
    Jefferys, Thomas, 47
    Ordnance Survey, **16**, 28, 29, 30, 37, 40, 47, **64**, 74
        packhorse tracks, 9, 76
        placenames on, 53
    Stansfield inclosure plan, **68**
    Towneley estate, 31

Marsden, Lancashire, xviii
Maxim, James, xvi
McAdam, John Loudon, 3
Mercia, 73
Mereclough, Cliviger, 28, 47
Metcalf, John, 41
Middle Pasture Farm, Cliviger, 66
Midgelden stream, Gauxholme, 29
Midgley, 17
milestones
    Allescholes, 8, 38, **50**
    Shurcrack, **50**
    Top Brink, Lumbutts, **50**
mineral extraction *see* hushings
Ministry of Transport, 5
monastic crosses, 47
monks' way, Whalley–Sawley, 11
moor gates, 6, 70
Moorbottom Road, Boulsworth Hill, 58, 66
Moorcock Road, Blackshaw Head, 51
moor-fence tracks, 71, **71**
moorland *see* wastes of the manor
Morecambe Bay, saltpans, 77
mosses, 40
    Red Moss, Cliviger, 44
motorways, 5, 75
Mount Cross, Shore-in-Stansfield, 47, 48
Mytholm, 53

N
Napoleon, 74
narrowgates, 6, 31, 58
National Parks and Access to the Countryside Act (1949), 80
national trail, 84
Naze Road, Gauxholme, **4**, 29, **37**
Neolithic routes, 46
New Forest, 76
Newsholme Dean cantilever bridge,

21, 46
Noahdale, 51
Noahdale Road, Stansfield inclosure, **68**
Norfolk, xv, 36, 37
Norman French, 73
Normandy, xvi
Normans, xvi, 3, 43
Norse, 73
North Hollingworth, Walsden, 30
Northallerton, 84
Northowram, 32
Northwell Lane, Heptonstall, **61**

O
Ogden Clough, Pendle, 42
Ogilby, John, xvi, xvii
Old Chamber, Hebden Bridge, 59
Old English, 73
Old Great Lane, Shore-in-Stansfield, 48
Old Scotch Road, Boulsworth Hill, **33**
Ordnance Survey, 74
  see also maps
overnight stopping places, 6, 63, 66
  Horsehold, Hebden Bridge, **65**
  Windy Harbour, Cliviger, 64
  Windy Harbour, Stansfield, **64**
Ox Lee Lane, Hepworth, **36**
Oxenhope Moor, 29
Oxford English Dictionary, 73

P
pack and prime ways, 2, 6, 27
packhorse bells, **xvii**, xxi, **xxi**, 32, 64
packhorse breeds, xix, 76
  see also Galloway
packhorse journeys, xviii, 6, 63
  effect of inclosure on, 71
packhorse load, weight of, xix, 75-6

packhorse routes
  antiquity of, xv, 5
  Blackstone Edge, xv, 66, **58**, 59, **59**
  Burnley–Halifax, 17, 19, 23
  Craven–West Riding, 29
  East Lee–Heptonstall, 19
  effect of reservoirs on, 72
  fragmentation of, 72
  Hebble End–Saddleworth, 64
  Heptonstall–Haworth, 29
  Holloway, London, **35**, 36
  Inchfield–Gauxholme, 29
  Lancaster–Richmondshire, 59
  Lothersdale–Saddleworth, xviii, 59
  Preston–Clitheroe, 17
  Rochdale–Elland, xv
  Rochdale–Halifax/Burnley, 8
  Rochdale–Hebden
    Bridge–Haworth, 37
  Shore-in-Stansfield–Heptonstall, 17, 66
  Todmorden–Burnley, 38, 52, 65
  Todmorden–Hebden Bridge, 53
  Trawden–Widdop–Heptonstall–Halifax, 25
  Watergrove–Inchfield, 29
  watering places, 62
  Whalley–Great Harwood, 59
  Whalley–Sawley, 11
  Whitewell/Bowland–Clitheroe, 11
  Widdop–Worsthorne, 40
  York–Chester, xv-xvi
packhorse tracks
  and inclosure, 69
  development of, 7
  guidebooks to, 87
  historical evidence for, 83
  maintenance by parish, 83
  on Ordnance Survey maps, 76
  restoration of, 86

Todmorden–Sourhall, 52
  trees along, 53
  tunnels on, 59
packhorse trade, xiv-xv, 5
packhorse trains, xvi, **xvii**, xviii, 2, 55
packhorse transport, xiv, 2, 73
  demise of, 6
  difficulties of, xvi, 3, 25
  distances covered, xviii
  effect of inclosure on, 71
  effect of weather on, 25
  hazards of, xviii, 7
  importance of, xvi, 49
  speed of, xviii
  vocabulary of, 73
Packhorse Triumph II, **xx**
packhorses, **xvi**, **xxii**, 2
  agility, xviii
  grazing for, 5, 62
  management of, xxi
  temperament, xx
packmen, 74-5
packponies carrying cloth, **xix**, **73**
packpony, Beamish, **63**
packsaddle, **xxi**
pannage *see* rights of common
parish duties, 4, 49
parish surveyor *see* highway surveyor
pasture *see* rights of common
Paul Clough bridge, Cornholme, **13**, 14
paved stream beds, 21
peat, 39, 42, 45
peatland, 27
  attempts to inclose, 44
  cairns as waymarks, 53
  difficulty of, 39, 40
  hazards of, 41
  moss, 40
  Pendle Hill, 42
  right of turbary, 44

varieties of herbage, 43-4
Pendle Hill, 34, 42, 52
Pennine Bridleway, 84, 87
Pennine Chain, 65
Pennine Way, 31
Pennines, 2, 33, 73, 76, 79
pikes, 52
piscary *see* rights of common
placenames
  on Ordnance Survey maps, 74
  salt, 65
Pontefract, 17
Pot Oven Farm, Cliviger, 58-9, **58**
prehistoric routes, 37, 46
Presgrave, John, 87
Preston, 84
Priestley, Thomas, xvi
private carriage road, **69**
private roads, 69
Psalters Lane, Sheffield, 77
public carriageway, 70
public inquiries, 82
public paths, 81
Public Record Office, Kew, 84
public roads, 69
Public Slake Trough, Stoodley, **62**
Pule and Standish common, 41

Q
Quarter Sessions, 84

R
Ragby Bridge, Inchfield, 29
railways, 5, 40
railway age, 6
Railway Mania, 5
railway records, 83
raised causeways, 31
Raistrick Greave, Widdop, 40, 72
rakes *see* causeways
Rake End, 30

Ramsden Long Causeway, **42**
  see also Long Causeway,
    Wardle–Watergrove–Inchfield
Reaps Cross, Heptonstall Moor, 31,
  40, **48**
Red Moss, Cliviger, 44
Reddyshore Scout, 8
Reddyshore Scout Gate, **37**, 38
reservoir records, 83
reservoirs, 72
Ribble valley, 79
Richmondshire, 59
Ridge Gate, Shore-in-Stansfield, 66
Ridgeway, 37
ridgeways, 36
right to roam, 87
rights of common, 67, 74
rights of way
  and inclosure, 69
  and inclosure awards, 7
  evidence of use, 82
  illegal closure, 71
  legal record of, 80
  loss of under the CROW Act, 87
  powers to extinguish, 71
  township lanes, 7
Ripponden, 66, 81
River Calder, 59
River Don, 17
River Hodder, 17
River Ribble, 73
River Trent, 17
River Wye, 15
road, 75
roadmending, **60**
roads used as public paths (RUPPs),
  81
Robin Cross, Burnley–Halifax Long
  Causeway, 47
Rochdale, 83
  cloth hall, 79

Rodmer Clough, Upper Colden, 77
Roebuck Inn, Portsmouth, 64
Roman Road, Blackstone Edge, xvi,
  31
Roman roads, 75
Rooley Moor Road, 34
Rossendale, 73
Rough Hill causeway, **39**, **44**
Rural Development Commission, 84
Rush Candle Clough, Black
  Hameldon, 44
rushes, 43-4
rushlights, 44
Ryder, Ruth, xviii

S
saddle bridges, 11, **11**
Saddleworth, xviii, 59, 64
saddling cotes, 66
salt pies, 77, 77
salt routes *see* saltways
salt trade, 65, 76
Salter Fell, 77
Salter Rake Gate, Lumbutts, **1**, **29**,
  30, 74
saltways, 8, 65, 76, 77
  on Ordnance Survey maps, 76
  overnight stopping places, 66
  Rochdale–Halifax, 66
Saxons, 73
Scandinavian settlers, 75
Scots, 74
Secretary of State for the
  Environment, 82
setts, 29
Shedden Bridge, Cliviger, 16
Shedden Drove Road (Worsthorne
  Road), Cliviger, **70**
Sheffield, 77
shelfway, **29**, **30**
Shepherd's Rest, Lumbutts, 30

Shurcrack milestone, Lumbutts, **50**
sighting points, 52
signposts, statutory requirement, 49
Slack Chapel, Heptonstall, 30
sled gates, 34
sledges, 19
snickets, 58-9
Hebden Bridge, 59
Lumbutts, 37
Pot Oven Farm, Cliviger, **58**
snow guides, 51
Somerset Levels, 45
Sourhall, Todmorden, 52, 65
South Hollingworth, Walsden, 66
South Pennine Packhorse Trails Trust,
59, 84-6, **84**
Supporters' Group, 86
South Pennines, 72, 83
Southampton, xviii
Sowerby, 32, 37
Sowerby Constables' records, xvi
spandrels, 12
speech, variation in, 73
spitalfields, 64
Sports Council, 84
Staffordshire, xvi, 17
stagecoach transport, 6
staircases *see* causeways, stepped
Stamford Bridge, 17
Standedge, 41, **85**
Standing Conference of South
Pennine Authorities, 84
Standing Stone Height, Cliviger, 47
standing stones
Devil's Arrows, Boroughbridge, 46
Stones, Todmorden, 46
White Slack Gate, **49**
stang poles, 8, 55, **55**
Stansfield inclosure award, 43, **68**
Stansfield township, 23
statute labour, 4, 5, 6, 23

Statute of Bridges (1531), 5
Staups Moor, Blackshaw Head, 17
Stephenson, George, 40
Stiperden, 24, 47
Stiperden Cross, 47
stone pitching, **85**
Stonecracker Joes, 60, **60**
Stones, Todmorden, 38
Stoodley Long Causeway, **27**, 37
see also Long Causeway, Langfield
Common
Stoodley Pike, **1**, 29, 51
Stourbridge Fair, xv
Stradford on Avon, xviii
Strathclyde, 73
streets, 75
Stump Cross, 47
surveyor of highways, 4
see also highway surveyor

T
Taylor, John B., 87
Telford, Thomas, 3
Thoresby, Ralph, 32
Thornton-in-Craven, 52
Thursby, Sir John, 16
Thursden, 25
Todmorden, 8, 38, 52, 65, 83
Todmorden Edge, 52
Todmorden Town Council, 84
toll roads *see* turnpike roads
tolls, xv
Top Brink milestone, Lumbutts, **50**
Top Brink pub, Lumbutts, 37
Top of Stairs, Oxenhope Moor, 29
Top Withens, 45
Tower Causeway, Todmorden, 38, 52
Towneley estate, 47
Towneley, Mary, 84
track, 75
trade routes, expansion of, 6

travel in seventeenth century, xvii
Trawden, 25, 58
Triumph II, xix, **xix**
Trough of Bowland, 77
trunk roads, 3, 5
trunk routes, 2, 75
tunnels, 59
turbary, right of, 44
see also rights of common
turnbyes, 60
Turner, Whiteley, 20
Turnhole Clough, Trawden, 58, **85**
turnpike era, 6, 75
Turnpike Mania, 5, 31
turnpike records, 83
turnpike roads, xvii-xviii, 4, 5, 54
Blackstone Edge, xvi, xvii
Burnley–Halifax, 19
Calderbrook–Walsden, 31
Wakefield–Manchester, 41
turnpike trusts, xvii, 4, 5
Turpin, Dick, 54

U
UK2000, 84
Upper Gorple reservoir, lost
causeway, **40**
urbanization, 80

V
Vancouver, Charles, xviii
volunteers, 84

W
Waddington, 11
Wakefield, 84
Wales, 73
walls, xv, **xv**
Walsden, 8, 28, 59
Warland, 38
wastelands *see* wastes of the manor

wastes of the manor, 67, 74
water catchments, 72
water damage, 59
water gates, 21
water troughs, 62, **62**
Watergrove, 28
Watersheddles Cross, **48**
Watson, Reverend John, xvii
Watty Lane, Gauxholme, 38
way, 75
waymarkers, 40
   natural features, 52
   prehistoric, 46
   statutory requirement, 49
Weasel Hall, Erringden, xviii, 59
Welsh, 76
West Riding, 40
   cloth trade, 79
West Riding County Council, 81

Westgate, Burnley, 75
Whalley Abbey, 47, 59
Whalley Nab, 59
Whernside, 39
Whirlaw, Stansfield, 64
Whitaker, Dr T. D., 73
White Slack Gate, 64
   standing stone, **49**
wiches, 65, 77
Widdop, 31, 40
Widdop Head, xviii
Wildlife and Countryside Act (1981), 81
William the Conqueror, 3
Wiltshire, 37
Windgate Nick, Addingham, 47
Windy Harbour, Stansfield, 64, **64**
Windy Harbour, Cliviger, 64
Withens, Erringden, 28

Withens Gate, Langfield Common, 51
Withersby, Janet, xviii
wool trade, xv, 47, 79
Worsthorne, 40
Worthorne Road, Cliviger, *see* Shedden Drove Road
Wuthering Heights, 45
Wycoller
   old causeway, **48**
   clam bridge, 46
   clapper bridge, 18
   packhorse bridge, 11, 17

Y
Yorkshire, xv
Yorkshire Street, Burnley, 75